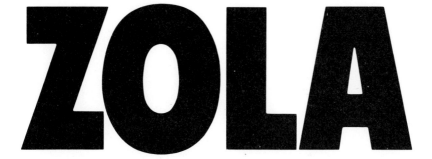

ZOLA

THE OFFICIAL BIOGRAPHY

Brian Vine with Zola Budd

D0416192

Stanley Paul

London Melbourne Sydney Auckland Johannesburg

Stanley Paul & Co. Ltd

An imprint of the Hutchinson Publishing Group

17-21 Conway Street, London W1P 6JD

Hutchinson Publishing Group (Australia) Pty Ltd
PO Box 496, 16-22 Church Street, Hawthorne, Melbourne, Victoria 3122
PO Box 151, Broadway, New South Wales 2007

Hutchinson Group (NZ) Ltd
32-34 View Road, PO Box 40-086, Glenfield, Auckland 10

Hutchinson Group (SA) Pty Ltd
PO Box 337, Bergvlei 2012, South Africa

First published 1984

© Daily Mail, London 1984

Set in 11 on 12pt Monotype Baskerville

Printed and bound in Great Britain by Butler & Tanner Ltd,
Frome and London

ISBN 0 09 159271 2

Acknowledgement

I would like to thank Neil Wilson, Athletics Correspondent of the
Daily Mail, for all his contributions and help.

ZOLA

Contents

A Star is Born

On Zola Budd's birth certificate, No. A926233 at the District Registrar's Office of the Republic of South Africa, her race is officially entered as 'blank', meaning white. This entry would dog her footsteps all her athletic life, because the world had ostracized her white-run homeland for its apartheid policy. If she had been black, maybe her escape to the outside world would not have been so difficult or so criticized. South Africa had been banned from international competition since 1976 by the International Amateur Athletic Federation, the ruling body of her sport, and had not been allowed to compete in the Olympics since 1960.

So here on the high veldt was the granddaughter of a portly, London process-engraver, moving through the bush around her home, barefoot, as fast as a gazelle.

A few weeks before she was to be secretly spirited out of her homeland to Britain, where she had historical rights to citizenship, Zola's relentless running took her up Naval Hill, past unflinching ostrich and leaping springbok with a faraway look in her misty green-grey eyes. She was dreaming of gold. Not the raw mineral which runs like a vein through South Africa, but the kind of gold fashioned into Olympic medals, the supreme accolade for athletes the world over.

Her whole person seemed to be consumed with this ambition as her spindly legs gobbled up thirteen miles a day in practice runs. Getting competition from the greats in her sport had become an obsession.

The heat haze rose around her to shimmer the spiky outline of the syringa trees. In the thin air of the veldt, 4568 feet above sea level, on ground scorched brown by merciless drought, this tiny young woman was in her element, as fresh as an English rose after a summer shower.

Zola held by her mother Tossie at her christening in Bloemfontein in 1966

Atop Naval Hill, a game reserve in Bloemfontein, Zola trains with shoes on with her coach, Pieter Labuschagne

Her birthplace was the only home she has known, but coursing through her reedlike frame she knew there was sufficient British blood to earn her a chance to prospect for Olympic gold. Bloemfontein, capital of South Africa's Orange Free State, was the backcloth of Zola's great dream, among the peaceful and majestic hills and ridges of the veldt.

A good deal of Zola's stamina today as a middle-distance runner probably comes from her mother's stout Voortrekker character. 'Tossie' Budd was christened Hendrina-Wilhelmena. Her grandparents were Dutch settlers; she the daughter of a farmer. Zola's birth meant a marathon labour for her, and on 26 May 1966 at Bloemfontein Hospital, a team of doctors had to put up an almighty fight to save Tossie's life which was endangered by haemorrhaging.

The trouble was that Baby Zola who today thrills and entertains the world with the speed of her legs had turned round in the womb before she was born. Bringing her into the world is remembered at the hospital as one of the more difficult births in its history. After delivery her mother had to spend the next three days half-conscious in a hospital bed betweeen life and death while doctors and nurses gave her endless amounts of blood.

Baby Zola was tiny, smaller than her brothers and sisters had been at birth. The nurses told her proud father Frank that she would be a 'stayer', though for days the family did not know if she would survive. Frank Budd had felt sure that the baby would be a boy, and had already chosen for him the unusual name of Zero. Frank decided to keep the 'Z' in his new daughter's name and call her Zola after the French novelist.

Zola was to grow up with all the positive attributes of a Gemini: restlessness, inquisitiveness, imagination and a willingness to experiment, hallmarks of others from her birth sign, like President John Kennedy and Jean-Paul Sartre, the existential philosopher.

As a child, she managed to combine Gemini experimentation with a dogged application to be the best, whether in the classroom or on the sports field. Her spare 6 stone 2 pounds today do not reflect the strength, control, and power that she brings to aggressive competition.

Her personality mirrors antecedents on both sides of her family and also the very place where she was born, Bloemfontein, a focal point on the veldt for the immigrant masses in the last century. Firstly, for people like her grandfather, Frank Budd, whose family had lived for generations in the East End of London; a gritty people used to taking the hard knocks of life. And on the other side, her mother Tossie, née de Swardt, of Dutch religious stock who came north on the Great Trek of the 1830s from Cape Province, where the British had the upper hand.

Her folk were pioneers, who faced disease and death and battles on the veldt with black tribesmen, to find a new life. The Budds' farm today is off a red dirt road from Route 30 outside Bloemfontein and consists of a substantial, airy single-storey house with English-style doors from the drawing-room to the garden, a red corrugated roof and plenty of animal life. Zola's zest for running began on the warm tarmac of Route 30, running the seven miles into town.

'She used to run on the road barefoot, but she found it ripped her feet to pieces, so she now wears shoes in training. Though she rarely wears them in competition,' says Frank, a quiet-spoken businessman with twinkling blue eyes.

Shunning spiked shoes wasn't a quirk.

'We were going through a bad time financially when Zola first started running and spikes were expensive. I believe she thought that if she didn't get us to buy them for her, that would be a contribution to the family budget. Now, perhaps it's psychological. She probably thinks she couldn't run as well with them and that there's no point in changing.'

Like every other teenager, Zola lives in chaos in her bedroom. One day she stuck a notice on her bedroom door rationalizing her untidiness – 'One of the advantages of being disorderly is that one is constantly making exciting discoveries' – signed A. A. Milne. It usually looks as though a hurricane has blown in through the open windows.

Drawers full of running shorts were left half open, clothes were scattered on the floor and bed, papers littered her desk where she was typing a thesis for her political science class at the local Orange Free State University, where she enrolled last autumn.

Zola congratulated by runners Sonja Laxton and Jeanette Grieve after breaking the world 5000-metre record on 5 January 1984 at Stellenbosch, near Cape Town

When she puts on her steel-rimmed school-marm specs, she becomes quite a blue stocking, though she has taken to wearing contact lenses in athletics – 'They've improved me because I can now see the running lines,' she chuckles. She matriculated last year with distinction in history, biology and business economics from Bloemfontein's Central High School, where her coach and Svengali Pieter Labuschagne teaches history to 14- and 15-year-olds.

The tidiest adornment in Zola's bedroom is a glass case hanging on the far wall. It holds a treasure chest of thirty-nine gold medals collected in her running career so far. To the side is a poster of marathon runner Alison Roe, and close to her bed are small pictures of this little teenager's heroes, British milers Steve Ovett and Sebastian Coe. And rather in the way that pathological generals keep a picture of their opposite number amid their war plans, Zola has a poster of America's glamorous middle-distance runner, Mary Decker, above her bed.

It was Decker's 5000-metre record that Zola broke on that blustery night at Stellenbosch, near Cape Town, on 5 January 1984. She recorded 15 minutes 1.83 seconds, knocking a sensational 6.45 seconds off the Olympic champion's time. Yet the fastest woman on earth at 5000 metres is a mere child.

A short report from the American news agency, Associated Press, carried by *The Times* in London on 19 October 1983, introduced the young slip of a girl to international headlines. The AP report, clipped, sanitized, impersonal and datelined Port Elizabeth, South Africa, carried racial overtones in its first two words, auguring the political storm to come.

It read: 'A white South African woman athlete, Zola Budd, who runs barefoot, has come within 2.39 seconds of the women's world record for the 5000 metres (established by Mary Decker) and is now considering a scholarship at the University of California. Her time of 15 minutes 10.65 seconds was set at the University of Port Elizabeth on Monday. Unless she changes nationality, Miss Budd will find American college athletics the only opportunity for serious competition.'

In Britain 'the Thunderer' was to keep abreast of this 'mighty atom' as South Africa was calling Zola, though none of her track competitors could manage as much.

On 6 January 1984, less than three months later, *The Times* reported from Reuter's, the famous London-based international news and financial agency: 'Zola Budd of South Africa clipped more than six seconds off the American Mary Decker's women's 5000-metre world record' in Stellenbosch, near Cape Town. Zola clocked a time of 15 minutes 1.83 seconds, against Miss Decker's

15 minutes 8.26 seconds. And the *Daily Mail*, which was to play such a vital role in Zola's career by bringing her to Britain, carried the first picture of Zola winning that race with a classic look of surprise on the timekeeper's face!

Her name was on every lip that night. 'Zo-la, Zo-la.' Like a tribal chant it followed her rhythmically round the Coetzenburg Stadium, rising and falling on the stiff sea breeze that plucked at the tiny figure.

On her mind were the last words of her coach, Pieter Labuschagne, 'Forget any record. It's not on in this wind.' But the thirteen thousand spectators were lifting her, urging her frail body forward past rival after rival.

On this night of destiny for 17-year-old Zola, it all seemed so easy. She lapped the track barefoot with the precision of a metronome, and the grace of a gazelle.

Each 400-metre lap averaged around a breathtaking 72 seconds. When 15 minutes 1.83 seconds flashed up on the electronic timekeeper and around the world, a star had been born.

The family was suddenly to live in the cruel white glare of unwanted publicity.

That night in Stellenbosch Zola gave the media a taste of her anti-celebrity style. She walked off the track at the Coetzenburg Stadium, closing her ears to photographers clammering for pictures and reporters bent on a statement, disappeared into the crowd, sorting out a young girlfriend to go and have a picnic in a field on their own.

Next day, she flew back to Bloemfontein. A star had been born internationally, even though her world-record time was not officially recognized because the International Amateur Athletic Federation ignores the performance of South African athletes as a result of the sports boycott. Back at the family farm where her father grows maize on his seventy-five acres, Zola's eldest sister Estelle, a jovial 27-year-old, baked her a cake in celebration and that made her happier than if someone had flown her to Maxim's in Paris for Krug and oysters.

As Frank says of the Budd house, 'We have a home that is lived in, not looked at. Zola doesn't make any demands. She is a home-loving girl.' There are just as many drawings and pictures of horses in Zola's bedroom as pictures of international runners. Riding is her second favourite sport – 'I just love horses,' she says. There are bays, greys and brown horses on her bedroom wall as well as a light bay she embroidered in wool and had framed.

'We had to send our only horse away to another farm,' confesses Frank. 'We thought Zola might go riding and hurt herself.'

She was offered a high-stepping American thoroughbred horse by a wealthy local breeder as a present for her record-breaking race. But because the Budds have always chosen to scrupulously observe the rules which guard Zola's amateur status, she regretfully had to turn the offer down.

In the hallway, Frank lifts the constantly ringing telephone. It's Puma, the sportswear giant, asking solicitously, 'Does Zola like our products? Has she signed with anyone yet?' In fact, she has been through and beyond the whole range of track shoes, and in any case has always bought her own.

Another call. This time a London agent, John Marshall, asks if he can fly out and talk to them and would Frank give him a verbal option on her career until he gets there. The answer from this highly protective head of the family was predictably negative.

John Marshall is better known for furthering the career of singer Nina van Pallandt and American pro-footballers than those of track stars. But the bandwagon, the entrepreneurs, think, is there to be climbed upon. Nina settled into a Hollywood career for a few years after Mr Marshall managed to get her some well-orchestrated publicity following her affair with Clifford Irving. Irving, you may recall, was the American author who went to prison over the writing of a hoax biography of billionaire recluse Howard Hughes.

Frank Budd had never heard of Mr Marshall, but has an instinct for what he does, right or wrong. He referred Marshall to an umpire of his affairs in Johannesburg, Bill Muirhead, a Yorkshireman who was to play a greater role in the Budd family's decisions as time went on. Up until their secretive flight to England, Zola's parents were always more interested in her day-to-day practice schedules and races than they were in the blandishments of entrepreneurs.

'We reckon we did about sixty miles a day in Zola's interests,' says Frank. 'By car, of course. Either Tossie or I went out with her on her twice-a-day runs and then we took her to and from the city a couple of times. She is a very determined girl. I remember she insisted on trying to make netball her sport when she was only about half the size of the other girls. She just wouldn't recognize that her physique wasn't right for the game. We had to get in touch with her coach, Pieter, to get him to talk her out of it.'

How It All Began

As a toddler, the spindly little legs of fragile, jut-chinned Zola Budd would carry her out of the reach of older children running in pursuit of her. 'She dived about like a hare, dodging them and turning round sharply,' remembers Frank. 'At three years and four years, she would race away from the taller girls.'

Frank Budd is a fiercely proud father. His shiny pate makes him look older than his fifty-one years. He is lean, tells a mean joke and remains apolitical in his politically troubled homeland. He has always shielded Zola from political questions – 'She doesn't even have the vote until she's eighteen' he will tell questioners, 'so how is she supposed to take responsibility for the things that South Africa is criticized for'?

All she wants to do is run, he maintains. And visitors who have said, 'Let her run. She can't help where she was born,' find special favour with Frank, who has lived with his daughter's tenacity on the sports field since she was a little girl.

'One day I collected her from school and she said, "I've just won two races". I just said "Good, you should always try and do that." But I never thought any more of it. Then she kept racing against her friends. She started to win diplomas at school for running. We still didn't think we had a "Wunderkind" on our hands. Never suspected that she would one day be voted South Africa's "Sportswoman of the Year".

'She has a tremendous steeliness underneath all her shyness – perhaps she gets it from me. But I know my girl and I knew she'd never be satisfied until she could run with her own class. I told her at breakfast after she ran in Port Elizabeth last March that I would move heaven and earth to get her to Britain.

'We had many offers from American universities, about ten in all. The University of Nebraska, the College of William and Mary, the two universities in Los Angeles ...'

Zola puzzles over the solitary candle in the cake celebrating her first birthday

In school uniform and cropped hair, aged six

But her father didn't think America was the right place for her shy personality. 'I find Americans too loud and brash – whenever you hear a commotion in the street in Bloemfontein with loud laughter, it's bound to be a bunch of American tourists.

'Sport is multiracial in South Africa. Some of Zola's running friends were black and our two black servants are devoted to her,' says Frank. 'She has always feared, I suppose, becoming a pawn of the politicians. She has no foes. All she wants to do is run and she always deserved to be given that chance.'

Zola spins on one toe like a teenager anxious to leave the room when asked about the political barriers set up against her country which prevent her from running in Springbok colours at the Olympics or in Europe.

'Apartheid and the other things began before I was born and

will probably be resolved long before I die,' she says. 'In the meantime, I want to run – and I will run with or against anyone, of any colour, anywhere, at any time and may the fastest win.'

'If my mother hadn't noticed that my toes pointed inwards when I walked, I might never have become a runner,' Zola now says, savouring the irony of the situation. 'I was twelve then and had never run a proper race outside school sports.

'The doctors found there was a little bone growing out of the instep of both my feet and these bones were forcing me to walk pigeon-toed. I couldn't have run like that. It seemed a big thing at the time to me but it wasn't a very difficult operation. I'm just glad my mother noticed when she did.

'Now my coach always points me out to the other girls as a good example of how to stand. He's often criticizing some of them for running with their feet pointing at "ten to two". That's funny because he runs that way himself. It makes me giggle.'

The girl who now has the world at her feet was talking in the sitting room of her family home, the farmhouse, seven miles from Bloemfontein.

She is surrounded by her best friends, a Manx cat 'Stompie' and wirehaired terrier, Fraaier ('in Afrikaans it means "prettier than anyone else" ').

Outside the French windows which she opens to get the smallest breeze from the flat veldt, peacocks strut beyond the steel perimeter fence. Geese gobble in the garden and a pet parrot squawks in the kitchen, swearing in Sotho, a native tongue.

Zola's home, a single-storey farmhouse on the outskirts of Bloemfontein

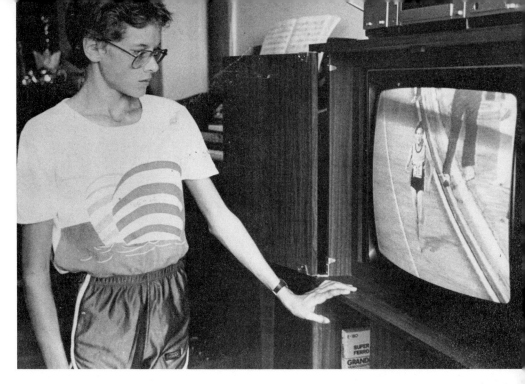

Above: At home in Bloemfontein, Zola plays the family's favourite video – her beating the world record for 5000 metres on 5 January 1984 in Stellenbosch

Left: With her pet terrier, 'Fraaier', at home in South Africa

'If I had not become a runner, I think I would like to have become a veterinary surgeon. I love animals. They are the things nearest to me. I'm often thinking of them when I run'.

The frisky terrier was a gift from an admirer after she broke the world record. So was a half-hundredweight heifer called 'Wisp-Will Kitty', a present from the local Cattle Breeders' Society.

Zola wasn't the least bit concerned when her gift cow bounded out of the truck and charged off at the presentation, startled by a bucket of cold water thrown over it by a helper. She is a country girl and was in her element.

From the other effects of her fame, autograph hunters, speeches, press conferences, and the spotlight of public attention, she shrinks with embarrassment. She is self-effacing to the point of withdrawal.

She was even too scared to make the one speech she wanted to make to the civic leaders of Bloemfontein, when they honoured her as the first recipient of an award for local achievers of special renown. Keys to the city, she pondered. 'I felt like saying

19

it would be better to give me the key to the city's running track. Getting into it is like getting into Fort Knox. But I didn't dare say so.'

Such are the small beginnings of this star, that back in Bloemfontein, Zola and her coach, high-school teacher Labuschagne, had to make do with a 400-metre track they marked out themselves between the rose bushes in the city's President Swart Park. On the park and on the sun-blistered tarmacadam roads across the veldt where she would train each day, Zola now wore running shoes to protect her multi-million-pound feet.

But on the smooth all-weather tracks where the public flocked to see her, she was always barefoot. Those bare feet and her long coltish strides became the hallmarks of this wonder child of the veldt. 'At primary school in Bloemfontein, almost all the girls ran barefoot and I just got into the habit. I'm always barefoot around the house, in the garden, everywhere – fortunately, I've never stepped on a snake!

'It was natural for me to run barefoot on the track. I only wear shoes when I train, because the sharp stones cut my feet. I did wear spikes once in an 800-metre race because it was raining and the track was slippery. Perhaps, at that distance, it made me a bit faster, but at the longer distances I prefer, spikes wouldn't help. I didn't even notice when the tracks were hot; we're used to that and my feet almost never needed any attention afterwards.'

If there is a certain sadness etched around the eyes of her mother Tossie, and a possessiveness over Zola by both parents, it might be traced to the grievous losses the Budds have had. Many years before Zola's arrival, her parents had reeled from the loss of Zola's elder brother Frank, who died aged twelve months from a liver defect, believed to have been contracted at birth. He would have been twenty-four now.

And tragedy struck again four years ago, when their eldest child Jennith, a bright and brilliant nursing sister, died after surgeons had operated on her arm for what they considered a malignant tumour. It proved to be non-malignant, and a mystery still surrounds her actual cause of death, though it was blamed on the kind of anaesthetic she was given.

'Zola was very close to Jenny,' said father, Frank. 'She took it hard when she died suddenly. She used to go running with her when she was small. They lived in each other's pockets. I have heard Zola say, "I'm now running for Jenny. I want her to be proud of me".' They are still a tight-knit family of four children, eldest sister Estelle twenty-seven, twins, Quintus and Cara, twenty-two, and Zola.

The Budd family's prize for a competition was a posed photograph: Zola stands between her parents, Frank and Tossie. At the back (left to right): sisters Cara, Jenny who died, Estelle and brother Quintus

Their home might well be in the heartlands of Afrikaans-speaking South Africa, but she was born the granddaughter of an Englishman. Her grandfather Frank George Budd was a Londoner, born at 129 Rushmore Road, Lower Clapton, London E5. Zola's maternal great-grandmother was also British: Janet McGibbon, daughter of Scottish parents from Falkirk and with a pioneer spirit, she was called 'Tom Cat' because of her fleet-footedness.

Janet came over from Britain 'on the boat' to nurse her sick sister, Margaret, who was married to a handsome British Army Captain, William Carding MC of the Royal Dragoons. He had been dispatched to South Africa at the time of the Anglo–Boer war. On her death Margaret told her sister Janet, 'marry Bill'. She did, and the captain and the second Mrs Carding adopted Bloemfontein as their home.

They settled on a farm at Weltevred, fifteen miles from the

city. The captain, Zola's great-grandfather, was a champion runner too, picking up many pieces of silver running for his regiment.

The family had many diehard British branches: Mrs Carding's brother Archie McGibbon, born in Gillingham, Kent, and brought up in Eire, was a club runner of some renown. During his career he became known as the 'Silver Bullet' at Moorfields club outside Dublin. His son Archie, now seventy-two, lives in Cape Town but Mrs Carding's three nieces – distant cousins to Zola – Mrs Eva Oldham, Mrs Elsie York and Mrs Mabel Chamberlain still all live in the same street in Leicestershire. Their father Edward Chamberlain, was wounded in the Boer War.

It was the Cardings' daughter, Joyce Carding, who met and married Zola's grandfather, Frank. He had arrived from London in Bloemfontein just before World War I, to fit a printing machine into the plant of the local newspaper, *The Friend*.

Putting in the machine took so long that he found himself trapped from returning to London by the outbreak of the 1914–18 War and stayed on to fall in love with and marry Joyce Carding, in Bloemfontein in 1926.

He described himself on the wedding certificate as a process-engraver but he was to start a career as a professional photographer for *The Friend*, taking photos of all the historical occasions, ranging from the building of the twin-towered city hall to the royal visit of the Prince of Wales. Off duty, Frank became quite a raffish man-about-town in his London brown trilby, enjoying a drink or two, and indulging in a passion for motorcycles.

There was plenty to focus his camera on.

His father-in-law, Captain Carding's soldiers continued to whitewash the stones of the giant White Horse built on the slopes of Naval Hill by men of the Wiltshire Regiment.

Lord Roberts, at the head of the British forces, had captured Bloemfontein from the Boers in 1900. The Boers had retreated without a shot being fired in order to save the city's historic buildings.

Above: Zola's grandfather, Frank Budd, at the farm outside Bloemfontein with his mother-in-law, Mrs Carding, at the wheel of a farm truck

Below: Janet McGibbon Carding, Zola's maternal great-grandmother (second from left) sits on the running board of the family car in South Africa. Mrs Carding was known as 'Tom Cat' because of her fleet-footedness

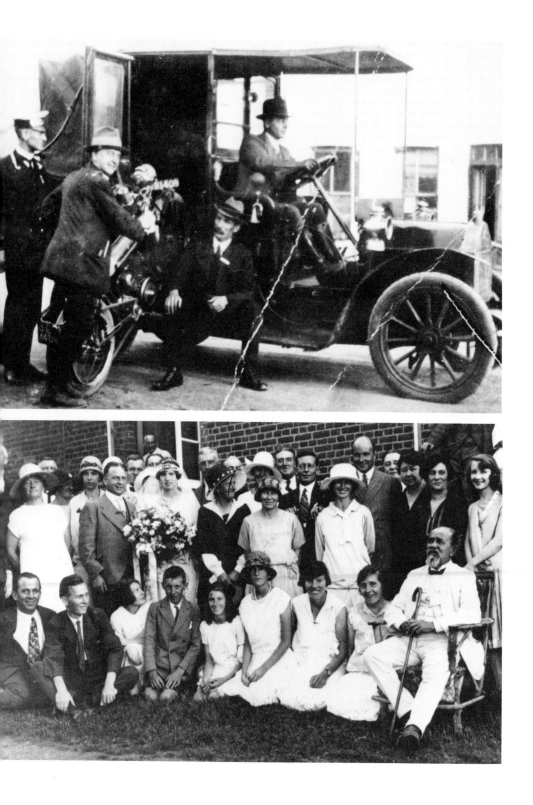

Above: Frank and Joyce Budd, Zola's grandparents

Right: Captain William Carding MC who settled in South Africa from Britain. He won silver ornaments running for his regiment, the Royal Dragoons

Opposite above: Zola's grandfather plays one of his practical jokes in South Africa – putting his motorbike in the back of a friend's car

Opposite below: Zola's grandparents' wedding reception in Bloemfontein in 1926

Zola's birthplace, the Orange Free State, had been settled by the Voortrekkers, the dour, hard-working farmers of Dutch origin who came north from Cape Province. Less than a quarter of a century after the Great Trek north the 'Free State', as it is abbreviated by the locals today, became an independent Afrikaans republic and twice it fought wars against the British. Long after the Boer War in which the Boer farmers of Free State joined together with Dutch settlers in the Transvaal to rebel, the Orange Free State in 1910 joined the Union of South Africa which had been formed as a self-governing part of the British Empire. But a final break with Britain was to come in 1961, when because of its racial policies South Africa was forced to break away from the Commonwealth and become an independent republic.

Zola Budd was to find herself a victim of the resulting political isolation of South Africa; its ostracism from the sports field and from world forums.

Zola's home town was founded by a Dutch Colonist, Johannes Brits, who built a house in the shade of a cool fountain, edged with exotic flowers – hence its name. Major Henry Warden, allegedly an illegitimate grandson of Bonnie Prince Charlie, bought land from Brits, put up a fort to protect British settlers and became the British resident.

Today, Bloemfontein's flowers and cool green parks are reminiscent of the remote splendour enjoyed by the early English settlers and the Dutch Voortrekkers who arrived in covered wagons hauled by oxen. Where Zola's feet carved a path this year on Naval Hill, antelope grazed peacefully, unaware of the passing of time. Once the Zulus and Matebele warriors indulged in a kind of genocide of lesser native tribes around these parts and Queen Victoria's second son Prince Alfred and friends slaughtered 5000 herd of animals on a game shoot here 125 years ago, but these are only memories of a dead past.

Within the family, Zola's father has always maintained this link to the 'old country' by insisting his children speak English at home, though out of lack of choice they attended Afrikaner schools. Zola was steeped in the English way of life. As a tiny girl, she remembers her parents returning from trips to Britain to see relatives. Frank went over a dozen times.

'The impression he gave me of England was of the cold, the greenness and the lovely parks,' recalls Zola. 'Of course, I miss South Africa. I certainly miss the weather and my brother and

Sporting portrait of Zola by her amateur photographer brother, Quintus

sisters. Before I came to Britain, I didn't know much about it beyond what I've learned in history classes and most of that seemed to be about the fights they had in South Africa.'

She is no dumb farm girl, she matriculated with three distinctions, one in history, from Bloemfontein's Central High School in 1983, and she earned herself a place at the Orange Free State University, studying political science and the native language of South Sotho.

She is often seen driving to the campus in a Bakkie, a second-hand pick-up truck she bought herself out of prize money paid into her trust fund, held by the South African Amateur Athletic Union.

This fund was later 'frozen' by the SAAAU, which felt childishly betrayed by her flight to a new land and future.

'The other day, I gave up my studies at the university because I found I couldn't concentrate on studies *and* running. Running is where my future lies and as my coach says, I can always go

Zola after winning a 10-kilometre race in her home town, Bloemfontein

Winning a 3000-metre race for juniors in Durban, South Africa

back to studying, but once I'm past about twenty-eight it will be too late to continue running.'

Last year (1983) alone, she won six national athletic championship titles, set five world junior records, and an all-African record, five South African senior records and was chosen as the country's Sportswoman of the Year.

She is unbeaten in races of 1000 metres and above since November 1981, a period in which she has won more than seventy races. She currently holds the world's junior records at 1000 metres (2 minutes 37.9 seconds), 1500 metres (4 minutes 5.81 seconds) – a time set in the thin air of the high-altitude veldt where performances are adversely affected) and 3000 metres (8 minutes 37.5 seconds). Her year culminated in her becoming the fastest woman on earth at 5000 metres, and although there is no 5000-metre race for women at this year's Olympics, there will be in the Olympics in Seoul, South Korea, in 1988.

Living all her life at Bloemfontein's altitude of 4568 feet above sea level, is thought to be one of the factors contributing to her phenomenal running ability. Like the Kenyan and Ethiopian black stars of long-distance running, who were born at similar altitudes in Africa, Zola's lungs have had to become more efficient than average, making the best use of the limited oxygen in each breath. Indeed, her times at high altitudes in Bloemfontein, Johannesburg and Pretoria, all cities high above sea level, suggest that even her best times now will come tumbling down as she runs more often at sea level.

'There is a fifteen-second difference between her best 3000 metres at high altitude and sea level,' says coach, Pieter. 'If she ever runs a 1500 metres at sea level, we might even see her beat four minutes.'

'I haven't run yet as well as I feel I can,' says Zola. 'Pieter and I think I can go a lot faster. My best will come at longer distances.'

Zola is a realist in her sport as well as being full of humility about her own achievements so far. Only months ago, Zola was saying, 'Mary Decker is out of my class at the moment. She's a great athlete, much more experienced than I and I wouldn't feel like racing her now. It would be silly. I know I've beaten her best 5000 metres time but then she's only run the distance twice. If she puts her mind to it I'm sure she could run it twenty seconds faster than she has. But, in time, perhaps I will too.'

From talk of future world records, Zola looks back to the way

Sprinting ahead of yet another field

it all began in Bloemfontein. 'I won my first race when I was five, an 80-metre event at my school, the Onse Rust Primary School, on sports day. I was always quicker than the other boys and girls when we played. But it wasn't until much later, when I came under Pieter's coaching at high school, that he made me aware of it.

'The first term at his school was the cross-country season. I hate cross-country. The ground in South Africa is too hard and so at the cross-country groups' training sessions, I didn't really try too hard. I was more interested in getting in the netball team with my friends.

'But Pieter's a man who gives you great confidence in yourself, and he kept telling me that I was a faster runner than any he had seen. I hadn't realized it but then I was only thirteen.'

Even at seventeen, childlike Zola has shown no wild interest in the normal teenager's loves of fashionable clothes, make-up and pop music. She says she's the outdoor type, quite content in shorts and T-shirt. 'Make-up? In the hot weather at home, it got all sticky and ran down my face. I don't wear it. I've got a few dresses, but I'm happiest in running gear.' Ask her about her favourite music and she'll say Brahms, but it's a genuine like, not an affectation.

It became apparent to all visitors that another secret of Zola's success as a world-class athlete was the combination of her relaxed family home life and her mother's English-style home-cooking, such as roast beef and Yorkshire pudding, rather than taut-nerve scientific training and a vitamin-balanced diet. One night she curled up on the dining-room floor with her grey cat after two hefty helpings of meat and proceeded to watch the violence of 'The A-team' on television.

'I don't have to worry about my diet. I eat what I like, because I burn it off running,' she said, dunking chocolate biscuits in her tea.

Her parents' favourite viewing are the video tapes of her past achievements. They are marked simply ZOLA and lie for all to see on top of the telly. She pretends to busy herself in her bedroom when the Budds proudly reshow her videos to guests and relatives. She stares ahead of her with the baleful look of a fawn – startled but unbowed and then gets on with her embroidery. She's in bed by nine, because she's always up for practice soon after dawn breaks.

Since her teens, Frank Budd has driven her into town from his farm for a 5.30 a.m. rendezvous each day at her coach's apartment. From there, it is only three hundred yards to Naval Hill and the ten-kilometre course through the game reserve on its table-flat top, where she runs under the gaze of springbok and impala.

'We had to run then because of the heat of the rest of the day. Pieter had to be at school by eight o'clock,' says Zola. Often, she would take breakfast with her eldest sister Estelle, at her apartment in town, before attending morning lectures at her university. She would be out running again on the veldt around her home in the afternoon and along the oven-baked roadway of Route 30 towards Bloemfontein.

Her slim outline, with her bony elbows swinging wide of her sides, is silhouetted against the hills in the distance. 'I am never frightened of people knocking me about in races. I think my sharp elbows would be good protection. One girl did try once. She cut in front of me using her elbows. She finished ahead of me, but they disqualified her.'

Behind Zola when she runs near the farm comes her mother in one of the family's cars. 'We never let her run alone,' says Tossie. 'She might fall or be attacked. You never know. She's still our little baby.'

Her father rejoices in tradition. He himself was trained in the dynasty-like traditions of the world of printing. He became a blockmaker, but he has owned businesses as a florist and private caterer, as well as taking over his father's small printing and process-engraving firm in Bloemfontein when he died. There, he has his eldest daughter, Estelle, in charge of the accounts, and his twins, Quintus and Cara, helping in the business. There are nine on the payroll.

Frank would sit as nervously as a father-to-be in his blue shorts and shirt, waiting for Zola's return from her afternoon run. His living room could be mistaken by its furnishings and knickknacks for a suburban house in Southend or Solihull. Because they remind him of his English descent, he has had a suite of heavy Victorian chairs and a sofa, inherited from an English aunt, re-upholstered three times. Today, the suite stands resplendent in eye-bruising blue, his favourite colour. It matches the brass lamp standard in the corner, with its blue silk shade edged in chintz, a 1940s British 'antique'.

The mantel shelf is cluttered with brass ashtrays – Frank smokes incessantly through a small black cigarette holder. Zola keeps reminding him that it's bad for the lungs, but he says it releases his tensions. Through the window comes a cacophony of barking from eight dogs and yelps from five puppies. Zola is returning from her run and a black ostrich in its acre-sized pen gazes at her progress through saucer eyes, pivoting on its long neck without moving its body. The Budds love birds, great and

Zola running barefoot in South Africa

small. Pigeons have a loft, sixty-five chickens flutter back and forth in the henhouse, and there are budgerigars.

From the time she was born, Zola's parents have called her their Laatlammethie, Afrikaans for 'Late Lamb'. But since her record-breaking run, she has had to grow up fast.

One shock was a proposal of marriage of convenience from a 65-year-old Birmingham man, Henry Allen, passed to her family through a newspaper. 'I found that very embarrassing as any girl would.' A day later one of the family's black servants asked, 'Miss Zola, you're not going to marry that old man, are you?' Zola's comment on this cheeky but well-meant offer to give her British citizenship was, 'I think I am too young for marriage.'

Though she could smash world records at will, she could not vote, could not drive a car alone and could not yet legally run a marathon, under Amateur Athletic rules, until her eighteenth birthday last May. And the marathon, not surprisingly, is the event in which she sees a great future for herself. All during her seventeenth year, her only concern was to find real opposition, whatever the distance. In South Africa, her only rival was the clock.

'Pieter says I have a clock in my head,' says Zola. 'I got so used to running against myself that I knew precisely what pace I was running. I never needed to look up at the track clock and still don't.'

The frustration of having no true opposition finally became too much for her. She had to run distances as short as 800 metres to find any South African with a chance of living with her speed and stamina. At 5000 metres she was in a class of her own.

It was on a night in Port Elizabeth, in March this year, when she accepted finally that her future lay overseas. That night, thirteen thousand turned up to see her attack her own 5000 metre world record, and groaned with disappointment when she ran only the fourth fastest world time of 15 minutes 9.86 seconds, averaging just below 73 seconds a lap.

'That really upset me. They had started to expect me to break records on my own every time I ran,' she said, after lapping all but one girl in the race. 'I felt I'd let them down. I knew I couldn't go on running this way. I had to go where there was competition, and Britain was the answer.'

To achieve that goal, she was willing to give up her studies, her home and her friends, and face even the unfair criticism of those who might use sport's innocent young stars to attack the policies of a government. Few athletes could have sacrificed so much that they hold dear for a chance to prospect for Olympic gold.

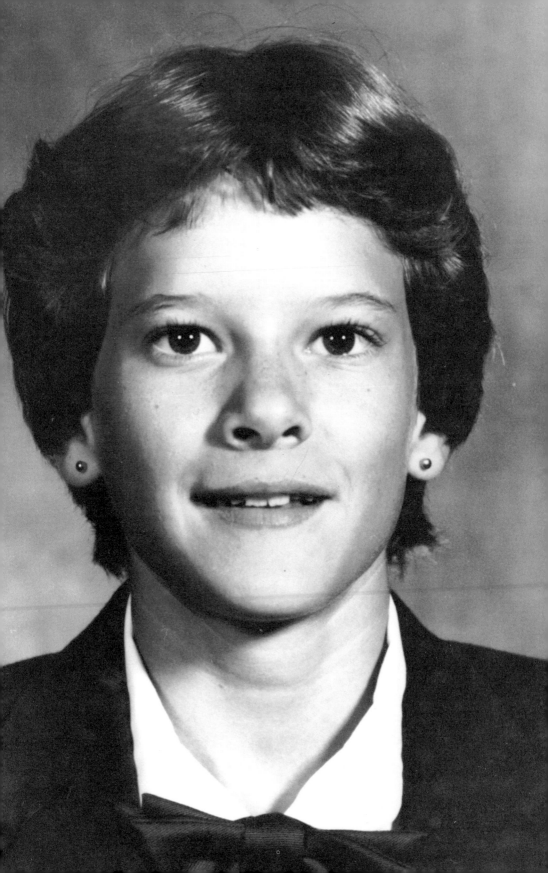

Who Made Zola Run?

Coach Pieter Labuschagne is a husky South African of French descent with a four-syllable name of which the two last syllables are pronounced like 'Cagney' with a guttural flourish of the tongue. He is brave and handsome, and a veteran of a couple of army spells fighting black guerillas on the South Africa–Zimbabwe border near the famous Beit Bridge. He is 6 feet 1 inch, fourteen stone with a roguish moustache to bring wisdom to his boyish face.

His handsomeness makes girlish hearts throb a little harder as he strides down the corridors of Sentraal Hoerskool, Bloemfontein's Central High School, where he taught history in Afrikaans to 14- and 15-year-olds. In his spare time, he voluntarily coached the girls' track and field team. He remembers thinking, when he first set eyes on Zola, that she didn't smile much or rag with the other girls or enjoy too many jokes. She had a face and bone structure set in a firm mould of concentration whenever she ran. Her grim expression, almost lip-biting, betrayed her intense determination and dedication. He calls her the most determined runner he has ever met.

Pieter was quickly to become more than a coach to Zola. He was the man she entrusted with all her confidences, her rarely imparted insecurities, her hopes and ambitions.

He was to orchestrate her coltish stride to a point where she would be unassailable in the length and breadth of the Republic of South Africa, and perhaps in future, the world. Her legs, from the beginning, flowed with a natural cadence and his job was rather like a singing teacher's, to coax the best out of her lungs and heart. And also to tap her courage and will to triumph. The man who made Zola Budd run once ran marathons himself. His nickname is 'Lappies'.

Aged seventeen in High School in Bloemfontein

Zola, the girl who now outruns the world, always wanted to be a netball player. 'She might have made the "D" team at netball,' chuckles Pieter. 'She was so small, she would have been knocked from pillar to post.' Labuschagne saw where her future lay the first moment he saw her run. That was in an inter-schools 1200-metre race. Zola was running for a rival school, the Willen Posthma.

'I noticed her because she beat one of my own girls out of third place. She was twelve and looked nine. But later, I asked my own girl who she was. A year later, the girl she'd beaten mentioned to me that Zola had transferred to my school, Bloemfontein Central High. So I asked her to join my cross-country group. She did, but made it clear that she really wanted to play netball. Her mother would see to it that she never missed my training sessions, but often she would hang around at the back of the field. She had this independent streak. She wanted me to know that it was she who would make the decision.'

Zola's determination to go her own way is now legendary in the Orange Free State. Defeats, rare and only at distances unsuited to her, must still be avenged.

Labuschagne, a 31-year-old who married fellow-teacher Caren three months ago, recalls one. 'She stopped in the middle of the State Schools cross-country championship to take off her shoes and only finished seventh. They picked the first six for the state team entered into the inter-provincial championships.'

So confident was Labuschagne that she could do better, that he himself entered her for the race as an individual competitor. She was thirteen. 'I remember vividly seeing through my binoculars this group of six in their Orange State vests and fifteen metres ahead of them, this tiny figure in the blue colours of her school – Zola. She beat the whole team.'

Since that day, he has been not only her coach – 'She believes in him like she believes in the Bible,' says her father – but also her closest confidant, classroom teacher, running partner, occasional chauffeur and second 'father'.

'Her father and mother haven't the contact with her that they had with their older children, because of the generation gap,' he explained. 'I live in her world of athletics and education. I know how she's thinking, her feelings and what she wants.'

It is more than pure coincidence that he is a graduate in political science, now writing a Master's degree thesis on Rhodesia from UDI to Independence and that Zola chose to study the same subject at nearby Orange Free State University. 'It's a subject she's always interested in talking to me about,' says Pieter.

How did he turn this tiny-boned teenager into a giantkiller of the track? He is modest about his part in the evolution of Zola Budd. 'Zola is a running machine. All I'm doing is improving the infrastructure, the capacity of the lungs and the efficiency of her body. Really, all I've been doing is improving the roads and rails within her.

'Somebody like me cannot drive a girl like this. She has to be driving herself, a self-motivator. Once she realized the improvement training was having on her there wasn't any stopping her. Now if I tell her to rest for two weeks, she's ringing me after three days, begging to run again. After a week, her mother is ringing too. Zola's impossible to live with when she's not running.'

He was a useful track runner himself as a younger man. But his association with her has not been without its personal humiliation. 'Zola beat my best for 3000 metres when she was only sixteen.' He has always been a disciple of the great New Zealand coach Arthur Lydiard, who produced the double Olympic champion of 800 and 1500 metres, Peter Snell with a schedule of long, slow-distance training. Under Pieter, Zola averages about thirteen miles every day, all of it at the same regular pace. Some of it was on the flat veldt, some up the dirt roads to the flat-topped hills around her home town.

'I have been holding her back. If I'm not with her in a car or running alongside, she trains too hard. If I tell her to do another two kilometres, she'll want to do five. If I say six sets of 800 metres, she'll do eight.' The potential of Zola is still untapped in his view. They didn't even have a proper training track at their disposal on a daily basis at home. They had been driven to marking out a 400-metre course between rose bushes in a local park. 'If she ever did any real track training, she would improve enormously. She broke the South African 1500-metre record last year without doing any track training.'

At thirteen, after the operation on both feet for the removal of a small bone in the arches, she broke her first track record, a schools state-wide age record. At fifteen, she broke a South African junior record, but her first major achievement came at the same age when she knocked an incredible 9.9 seconds off her own best for 1500 metres with a time of 4 minutes 9.1 seconds, just half a second away from the South African senior record. That won her national Springbok colours. Then records started to tumble to her.

So what makes her the great runner she is? Scientists say she is a heart–lung machine on legs. At Cape Town Medical School, Dr Tim Noakes, a sports scientist, describes her as one-in-fifty-million. 'She cannot be compared with the normal person,' says the doctor. Pieter has sent her to the local university's medical centre for a VO2 test which measures how efficiently the heart and lungs use oxygen. 'They said she was exceptional,' is all he will say.

He has avoided other uses of scientific methods to improve her. 'Much of her success is down to Mum's cooking and Dad's physique – she has the same legs – and determination. The only supplement I give her are iron tablets each day. We have success. Why change it? Perhaps when she's older we can be more scientific. What bothers her most right now is putting on weight. I say to her, "Look at yourself, you're like your Dad. You'll be skinny all your life." I try not to interfere with what nature has given her. I try to understand her, how she's behaving and thinking and between those narrow lines I'm coaching her.'

Amazingly, she has never suffered an injury which has stopped her running. In the four years he has coached her, the only illness she's had was two-day 'flu. Only rarely does she even need to put sticking plaster on her feet after her barefoot racing.

Pieter is the first to admit that his protégé is shy and introvert. 'I think running is her way of expressing herself.' But there is a tough independent streak, too. 'Promoters used to want her to wave to the crowd. She says it isn't necessary. That's how she is – independent-minded. She will do it her way.

'She doesn't want to be a star. She finds being a celebrity very difficult. One day nobody had heard of her; next day, reporters from all over the world were at her doorstep. It would be difficult for any young person to cope. But Zola is holding up well. It bothers her but she is not letting it show. We have had to think of ways of escaping the problem of autograph hunters. We were planning to have autographed postcards of Zola printed and instead of her having to stand and sign for hours on end we'd just hand out these cards.'

Zola is so modest that she did not at first like that kind of grandiose gesture. 'She considered people might think her big-headed. But it has reached the stage where she just can't please everyone. Zola just loves to run. No one pushes her. She doesn't have to steel herself to go out and train every day. In fact, before now her father has had to talk her out of running too far. She's come a long way already, but she still has a long way to go. I don't think she'll break down. Her programmes will be carefully plotted.'

Because of the closeness of their partnership, they almost always trained together in South Africa. When they got to Hampshire and to Surrey, their twice-daily training session remained sacrosanct.

Above: Making her British debut at Dartford

Right: At Crystal Palace, Zola glides into the lead in her second race in Britain

Below: In early morning sunshine, Zola has a curious audience of ostriches as she practises on Naval Hill, Bloemfontein

Smiling proudly, Zola holds up her new passport which followed the granting of British citizenship by the Home Office

The day after her athletics debut, Zola sees her name in the Sunday newspaper headlines at the offices of the *Daily Mail*

Against the backcloth of the Houses of Parliament, where later there was to be both criticism and praise of her, Zola takes the air

Minutes before her debut at Dartford, Kent – a new British athletics star is about to be born

Left: On her bed, Zola cuddles her cat, Stompie, and behind her is American athlete pin-up, Mary Decker. Zola was pictured at her father's farm in South Africa

Above: Zola greets one of the pet ostriches on her father's farm outside Bloemfontein

Below: The Budds at the farm with their household staff

Sacrifice is what Zola has meant to Pieter, an archetypal Corinthian. He would delay moving into his first marital home, temporarily leave South Africa and take six months leave of his job to launch her on the road to her Olympic destiny.

'If you are working with a girl as talented as Zola you'll do anything to see potential fulfilled.'

Zola aged sixteen practises in shoes at Bloemfontein wearing her High School colours

After beating her one-time arch rival Stephanie Gerber in South Africa

'Nationality Games'

Just when Zola Budd should have had a song in her heart with her world-record achievement for women over 5000 metres on that windy night in Stellenbosch, she was becoming morose because of the ostracism of her country from international sport. It is difficult to console an achiever when all opposition at home has been flattened and she knows that the only competition to improve her times has been forbidden to run against her. Father could do little to lift her heart – though without fully realizing it he embodied, literally, her passport to international competition.

Since the sports boycott against South Africa, her fellow South Africans have had to resort to all sorts of changes of nationality in order to get themselves to Olympiads since South Africa stopped competing in 1960.

The 'Nationality Games' had become an indelible part of the Olympic Games shenanigans. It was a crueller extension of the shamateurism controversy as to whether athletes today, with their enormous sums of money from sponsors for everything from running shoes to gift homes, meet the amateur ideals associated with the Olympics.

Typical of the 'nationality' roundabouts was the case of South African 800-metre runner Marcello Fiascanaro, now thirty-five. He was offered Italian citizenship by Rome in 1973, the year he achieved a South African record for his distance of 1 minute 43.7 seconds. He was born under an African sky, but his parents were migrants from Italy. Under Italian colours, Marcello enjoyed a good career in Italy, but a foot injury barred him from his ultimate objective of running for gold at the Montreal Olympics in Canada.

There are dozens of cases of Zola's fellow countrymen competing in Olympics under 'flags of convenience'. Far from being shamed by that expression, they feel that it is sporting hypocrisy to ignore the achievements of a whole nation of athletes and that it is cruel and inhuman punishment for them to have to bottle up talent which could overturn the world-record books – as Zola has done – by an arbitrary stroke of the pen. South Africa's Amateur Athletic Union was expelled from the International Amateur Athletic Federation in 1976 for being in breach of its constitutional ban on discrimination on the grounds of race and colour.

Even as Zola contemplated her next move on the sporting chessboard – as a minor she had a right to British citizenship because of her father's own British-born father – a High Court case was being fought in London by South Africa's Amateur Athletic Union. South Africa claims that the expulsion from the IAAF was illegal under its own constitution. That demanded a two-thirds majority vote. The motion achieved only a bare majority. So concerned were the IAAF that the case might be lost that at one stage they were farcically considering moving their headquarters from London to Rome. Italian law would be less helpful to the South African case and far more time-consuming.

Since the writ was first served in 1983, the international body has played for time. Most recently, it asked for the constitutions of every athletics club in South Africa. 'They wanted us to provide the evidence to convict ourselves if the High Court ordered our re-admission on a technicality,' laughs Chris Botes, General Secretary of South Africa's AAU. The constitutions would fail to help the IAAF's case. Every South African club, with the exception of those in one-race universities, is now open to all.

If the AAU wins its case before summer's end, the IAAF would be faced with the humiliating prospect of having to allow AAU athletes to compete at Los Angeles, with a resulting retaliatory boycott by the black and Eastern European nations which dominate its voting, if not its championships. 'The funny thing is that they have amended their own rules since kicking us out, to make it more difficult to suspend a nation,' says Botes. 'If we get back in they will find it hard to get us out again.' Though that doubtful victory would be won on a legal technicality, the South Africans believe it is justified by the physical evidence. All discrimination has gone from AAU rules since it abolished its separate organizations for blacks and coloureds in 1977. Now its vice-president, Edward Setshedi, is a democratically elected black; two other blacks have won election to its coaching committee, one to its cross-country committee and three blacks are employed as national coaches. When a town council, Kempton Park, near Johannesburg, banned mixed sport at club level on its municipal grounds, the AAU retaliated by boycotting the town's tracks.

What angers the South Africans is the Western hypocrisy. For years, nobody outside South Africa gave a thought for the athletes there, the real victims of bans. They were just casualties in a political war, of no more concern to governments than the Americans deprived of their 1980 Olympic places by President Jimmy Carter's boycott of Moscow over the Afghanistan invasion.

In private talks all that Britain's athletic authority considered necessary to allow Zola to change to the running colours of red, white and blue, was a different passport. Even the IAAF said initially that they would raise no objection once she had any passport other than a South African one.

So what difference, cynics ask quite reasonably, does a piece of paper make to the athletic authorities? Does it change her from the victimized wisp of a girl she was without it? Does it make the world-record times she has run any more real? This 'Trojan Horse' of convenience – changing her nationality – plainly ridicules the principle at the core of the boycott.

The anger of South Africans had turned to cynicism. Every day in Bloemfontein, the Budds passed by the grand offices of Prudential, of Legal and General, of Barclays Bank, and wondered what made sport so special that it was singled out as a way of condemning generations of the young to isolation at the bottom of the world. What more, they ask plaintively, can they do? A Springbok rugby union team, once the embodiment of white supremacy, has a black coach this winter (1984). They have fielded black players; famous white clubs like Johannesburg's Wanderers have thrown open their doors to all.

All but three of the twenty-six summer and winter Olympic sports are controlled in South Africa now by single multiracial bodies, and the other three promise to change the day any black or coloured bothers to take them up. And so keen have the South African Government been to clear sport of the charge of discrimination, that they have removed the word totally from all legislation and abolished the Ministry of Sport.

Yet South Africa is still a sporting outcast. 'IAAF members have admitted to me that it's not changing our sport which will satisfy them, but changing the policies of our government,' says Botes. The world, it seems, is happy to visit South Africa when the money is right. Cricketers, boxers, tennis players, golfers, Formula 1 drivers and jockeys are all regulars. Professional heavyweight champion Gerry Coetzee, 'the great white hope', was scheduled to be welcomed in America this year to fight black world champion Larry Holmes.

Even England's controversial rugby team will be welcomed

back to Britain later this summer, if they have triumphed over the Springboks in their own backyard. The last victorious team, another which ignored the boycott, was welcomed home at Heathrow Airport by the then Labour Minister of Sport, Denis Howell, a politician who was to cause a stir over Zola. Since it was his government that signed the Gleneagles Agreement in 1977 which prohibits Commonwealth contacts with South Africa, the irony of his greeting Britain's conquering rugby heroes was not lost on the high veldt.

Those whom the boycott hurts are those most vulnerable, those who play their individual games for the love of them, the runners, jumpers and swimmers. They might as well have a contagious disease. The only accepted cure is a change of passport.

The last place on earth the International Amateur Athletic Federation would expect to find South Africa's athletes would be in the Coliseum in Los Angeles at this year's Olympic Games. But as a group they will be there, albeit in the stands. Twelve superbly fit runners, picked at official trials in the republic and all qualified according to the IAAF's official Olympic standards, will be chosen for the trip of a lifetime to Los Angeles. All will proudly wear the green blazers and Springbok badges awarded as the highest honour in South African sport. All will have prepared as well as any Briton or American for their event.

But of course none of them will take a single step on the Olympic track. They will watch frustratedly from the stands as ticket-holding spectators, a symbolic protest by victims of the world's stubborn refusal to play games with South Africa. One place on this 'ghost' team was reserved for Zola, the girl whose world-record-breaking performances reopened the Western world's eyes again to the poor pawns of sports politics.

In an outraged show of defiance, South Africa's AAU will send their team anyway, the first since the International Olympic Committee made them unwelcome guests at its four-yearly party. 'They have earned their chance to at least taste the atmosphere and spirit of an Olympics,' says General Secretary Botes. Other South Africans are due to compete in Los Angeles in the names of the United States, Israel, Switzerland, Botswana, Portugal and West Germany. Four of the athletes are holders of national Springbok colours, just like Zola.

One will be a new US citizen, Sydney Maree, a black runner from Mamelodi, near Pretoria. Though he left his native South Africa in 1979 to take up a sports scholarship in America, he was only awarded his US citizenship on 1 May, less than three months before the Olympic Games. Such is the cynicism employed in the 'Nationality Games' capers. The Americans did a quick shuffle to see him awarded resident alien status on arrival and handed him a passport so that he could run for the United States in the 1981 World Cup, even though he still had not been sworn in as a citizen.

Maree, who set a world record for 1500 metres in 1983, saw Zola at a splendid sports dinner in a Johannesburg hotel less than a week before she secretly left her homeland. The colour of their skin was all that divided them in their resolve to go anywhere they could fulfil their potential. There were knowing glances between them, when they were reintroduced. Something seemed to tell Maree that it would not be long now before Zola showed a clean pair of heels to South Africa, and end the frustration of just simply running against a stopwatch.

Springbok middle-distance runner Mark Handelsman, twenty-three, expects to be selected by Israel for the 800 metres at the Olympics. Handelsman is of the Jewish faith and worked on a kibbutz in Israel in order to qualify as an Israeli. His birthright and citizenship were wholly South African with his parents still residents of Johannesburg, but he claimed an entitlement to an Israeli passport and spent the summer of 1984 polishing his running prowess which at one time made him South Africa's leading 800-metre runner.

After a three-month stay in Portugal in the summer of 1983, Springbok steeplechaser John da Silva, a physical education graduate of the University of Port Elizabeth where Zola has often competed, won Portugal's national steeplechase event. He was quickly chosen to represent his father's country in Los Angeles. The unexpected accommodation was hallmarked for its speed, rather than his overriding claims to be Portuguese.

Agreed, white South African 28-year-old world-class javelin thrower Koos van der Merwe is more likely to be mistaken for a German than a Chinaman, but his claims to West German citizenship are clouded in mystery. Nevertheless, he suddenly became a West German citizen last year, after studying at a local university and in the time it takes to throw his javelin, he was guaranteed a place in the West German Olympic team for Los Angeles.

Van der Merwe is the sixth-best javelin thrower in the world, with a 91.24-metre South African record – though again this record, until now, has been unrecognized by international sporting bodies observing the sports boycott of his native country. Nevertheless, it explains why the Germans were quick to leap in with the offer of a passport and all the javelins he needs. His parents still live in Pretoria, the Afrikaans-speaking seat of the Botha Government.

A black Springbok, Matthew Moshwerateu, who holds the South African 5000- and 10,000-metre records will be adopted by Botswana for his attempts at the Olympics. He went away to university in the United States in order to get the kind of competition he requires to be among the best distance runners in the world.

Cornelia Buirki, formerly Cornelia de Vos, from the early English settlement of Port Elizabeth, was voted Swiss athlete of the year for the eighth consecutive year in 1984. Though born in the Cape, she now runs for Switzerland in the Olympics as the wife of a Swiss businessman, Jorg Buirki. She went to the last Olympics in Moscow on the Swiss team and she also ran for Europe at 1500 metres and 3000 metres at the World Cup in Rome in 1981. She may be Swiss by adoption, but South Africans still proudly think of her as their own and she returns home each winter to carry out her training in Port Elizabeth. Her 3000-metre record is paradoxically nine seconds slower than Zola's, when the Young Pretender was still looking to Britain to adopt her.

Julian Marsay didn't need to apply for British citizenship like Zola, when the boycott looked like bottling up his athletics career. He was born in Leeds and came to South Africa as a small boy with his British émigré parents. After he notched a new South African 3000-metre steeplechase record with an 8 minute 22.6 seconds time, Julian became Olympic material. He went back to Britain with his British passport to train for the Moscow Olympics, but eventually wasn't quite good enough to make the team.

The challenge from Labour's ex-Minister of Sport Denis Howell, about pressure being exerted on Home Secretary Leon Brittan to facilitate a British passport for Zola, was later weakened by a skeleton in the former minister's cupboard.

In the House of Commons, Mr Howell lambasted the Home Office and the *Daily Mail*, who brought Zola Budd to Britain to take her rightful place among her sporting peers with a passport to which her direct ancestry gave her legal right. Home Office Minister David Waddington replied to his charge that her application had been speedily dealt with: 'If she had been left in the queue, the delay would have denied her the opportunity to compete for a place in the Olympic Games. The cry then would have been that Home Office bureaucracy would have denied a 17-year-old girl a great chance in her life.' Waddington went on to make mincemeat of Howell's objections, adding: 'What the Right Honourable gentleman is saying, is that if he had been in office he would have blown his beastly whistle. I believe I talk for the whole country when I say that he would have deserved to have choked on the pea.'

The skeleton not produced from Howell's locker was an incident fourteen years previously, when heavy pressure was used to get a certain foreign sports personality British nationality. Exerting the pressure at the time was the then Minister of Sport – Mr Howell. Angelo Parisi was born in Italy in 1953. His family was not of British stock. As far as anyone could tell, he had a proud Italian line running back to the days of ancient Rome.

In 1970 Parisi, whose parents emigrated to England in 1958, wanted British nationality so that he could represent Britain in judo at the European Judo Championships. The law said that he could not apply for a British passport until his seventeenth birthday, two months before the championships were due.

Howell leant on the Home Office. Parisi received his passport in twenty-four hours, won the heavyweight title in those games and went on to win an Olympic bronze medal for Britain in 1972. Ironically, the Parisi campaign backfired on Howell. For Angelo proceeded to marry a French girl and changed nationality for a second time. Representing Britain's old foe, France, in the 1980 Olympics, he won a gold! He will represent France again in Los Angeles.

So ludicrous has become the struggle of South African athletes for an Olympic anchorage, that long-distance black runner Vincent Rakabele, who runs the mile for South Africa's Bracken Gold Mine, may become a one-man Olympic team for Lesotho, the former British protectorate of Basutoland. Rakabele represented Lesotho in the marathon at the 1980 Olympics in Moscow, but this time they have too few contestants for the games and a hard-pressed budget.

The spiked shoes brigade are not the only South Africans who have sought to acquire foreign nationalities in order to play sport in other countries of the world. Cricket heroes Alan Lamb and Chris Smith were in the 1983/84 MCC team which toured New Zealand and Pakistan, and Kepler Wessels went to play against the black West Indies teams as a member of the Australia XI.

Clutching an English spring flower and pondering the future

In Demand

It was on 6 March 1984, that the *Daily Mail*'s award-winning sports columnist Ian Wooldridge described Zola Budd as 'the hottest property in world athletics'. His words were to reverberate round the globe. After Zola's slashing of glamorous American Mary Decker's 5000-metre world-record time by a 'monstrous' $6\frac{1}{2}$ seconds, as Wooldridge called it, the race was on for her signature.

'Her birthright ties, though tenuous, are British. Her paternal grandfather, Frank George Budd, was born in Hackney, London, on 4 February 1886. He emigrated to South Africa early this century taking with him some heavy pieces of furniture which are regarded as heirlooms in the Budd household to this day. But one grandfather and a few sticks of furniture are not enough. Which is why, for the past nine days and possibly for weeks to come, remarkable diplomatic moves are happening to gain Zola a British passport and the right to run for Britain in the Olympics.'

The race to handle Zola was already well into its stride at the time of Wooldridge's writing. The cream-coloured telephone, Bloemfontein 38858, trilled in the hallway of the farmhouse home of Zola. Naude Klopper, a kingpin businessman in Johannesburg, was on the line for Frank Budd. 'It's about Zola,' explained Klopper. 'Don't you think she should meet a good agent like Mark McCormack?' The phonecall began the race to capture the signature on a contract of the track star, the best woman athlete in South African history.

Frank, her father, had never heard of McCormack, the American international super-agent, whose clients range from Bjorn Borg through veteran golfer Arnie Palmer, to Captain Mark Phillips and up to the Vatican, on the Pope's visit to England. The Budds may be simple rural folk with English ancestors on both sides of Frank's family, but all are highly intelligent and strongwilled, and not least Zola, despite her will-o'-the-wisp build.

There is a tungsten quality beneath their country-cousin exterior. Frank, now restlessly wanting the very best for his daughter's world-class talent listened to Klopper. After all, he was the man who became a patron of another South African runner, Sydney Maree, whom he financially aided to international stardom. Klopper became Maree's Svengali in the late seventies. He bought the dirt-poor black athlete running gear, track suits and financed his travel to competitions all over the republic. Later, he advised on scores of offers of sports scholarships coming from United States universities. And to escape the sporting boycott against the country of his birth, Maree took an offer from America's Villanova University and once there, applied for US citizenship.

While the four-year process of naturalization went on, he was allowed to run and his performances were so outstandingly that in 1981 he was picked for the US team at the World Athletics Cup in Rome.

It was the same year that he became one of the exclusive clients of McCormack, founder of the International Management Group, whose headquarters are in Cleveland, Ohio. McCormack's skill at targeting on to the right big names is firmly indicated by his cable address: Marksman. Now Zola Budd, the waif from the veldt, was in his sights. Her father was invited to fly to Johannesburg to meet McCormack in his hotel suite to discuss Zola's career, together with her dilemma over the sports boycott, which was bottling up any appearance on the world stage of athletics.

'At first, I thought he was a sponsor,' recalls Frank. 'I didn't realize until I saw him that he would want to be her manager. He was in South Africa on some kind of golfing event, but he told me management was his business. I told him that it was too early in Zola's career for her to be tied to a huge management contract and that it was something we might want from his organization down the line. He was pretty persistent and said that he would send one of his staff out to see me and explain the whole business in greater detail.'

A few days before meeting McCormack, Frank had gone to Johannesburg to talk with the affable Yorkshireman Bill Muirhead, the Group Marketing Head of Defy, a domestic appliance company. A mutual friend had put them together. Their meeting had gone well and ended not in a contract, but an honourable handshake. Frank was looking for some sponsorship for Zola's burgeoning career. Small beer really: expenses for transport and hotels so that he and Tossie could continue to follow her around the far-flung running circuit, which sometimes meant hundreds of miles by car and hotel bills and costly flights from Bloemfontein to Cape Town or Port Elizabeth. In exchange, he agreed that Zola, he and the coach would wear the Defy logo on their blazers.

McCormack continued to express interest in Zola's career and promised to send one of his lieutenants, a likable Englishman, John Simpson, to follow up on their talk. Simpson went to the Budd farmhouse outside Bloemfontein, and the father explained that huge sponsorship and money was not paramount to Zola's career. They were just looking towards a British passport which could be granted to her at the discretion of the Home Secretary under the Nationality Act.

Frank told the saga of how his father was born in London, and came to be trapped in South Africa just before World War I. Simpson promised Frank he would try to achieve British status for Zola, as Frank was entitled to a British passport. The corridors of power were awoken to Zola's plight but Frank thought they were moving all too slowly and painfully for the girl who knew in her heart that unless she moved country, her athletics career could be damned by apartheid.

He made a confidant out of Defy's marketing chief Muirhead, who speaks with the accent of his native Yorkshire though he has worked around the world, including sixteen years for industrial giant Unilever. Mr Muirhead is a blunt and frank fellow, who puts a heavy emphasis on honour in business. Soon he was to have Zola Budd on the phone at his sixth-floor offices of a shopping centre on the outskirts of Johannesburg, consulting him. Dad would phone too.

Frank quickly made Bill an arbiter of what they should or should not consider to allow Miss Budd's international career to bloom. All the time, the family maintained its public position, that Zola would not forsake her country for British or American status. Meanwhile, moves were being made behind the scenes. Simpson of IMG was now telephoning the offices of Defy because of Muirhead's key role as an adviser to the Budd family.

On Bill's office wall was a reminder of the British way of life – a photograph of his wood-beamed home at Stratford-on-Avon, Warwickshire. Defy itself is three quarters owned by a Birmingham company, Glynwed. It employs 5000 people, the majority of them blacks in South Africa with plants and offices in Johannesburg, Durban and Newcastle, making appliances from stoves to washing machines. The US General Electric Company have a stake in Defy too.

'If Britain doesn't come up with a passport for Zola, I would have to advise the family to go to America and accept one of the university scholarships,' said Muirhead in one of his more exasperated moments. He travelled to and from his farmhouse home in an exclusive white suburb of Johannesburg at the wheel of his Mercedes, not knowing what news the post would hold for the Family Budd each day.

Already in London the die had been cast for the *Daily Mail* to take a decisive hand in the plight of Zola Budd. Editor Sir David English called for a bold approach to the family. The newspaper would extend a hand of friendship to the Budds and advise them to the best of its ability what course to follow, in order for them to apply for Zola's British citizenship.

Special Correspondent Brian Vine and the *Mail*'s Athletics Correspondent Neil Wilson were dispatched on the British Airways night flight to Johannesburg. It was an important flight, because Zola was running the next evening in Port Elizabeth and Vine had made a date with Frank Budd by telephone to meet him at his seafront hotel a few hours before she ran her last 5000-metre race at the local university track.

The excitement did not die down for the seventeen days it took to forge a trust between all parties. Because Zola possessed such a unique talent, she had been inundated with offers from countries round the world. Italy was very keen to offer her citizenship. But the greatest pressure had come from the United States. With its tradition of offering scholarships to athletic sporting talents of the world, America was determined to get Zola. Bill Muirhead was in charge of sorting through the offers of the finest campus facilities and the best coaches. And, of course, easily facilitated US citizenship.

Vine shuttled between Bloemfontein and the city of Johannesburg to see Muirhead. Wilson went on sporting sorties with Zola. All the time, a trust was being built up between the Budds and Sir David's envoys. Time was running out though, because from Zola's eighteenth birthday, 26 May, her British citizenship application would not be processed as that of a dependent child – even if discretionary powers were used. For an adult it could take three years to come through, ruling out the 1984 Olympic Games.

For all her shyness and humility, Zola is a pragmatist. She had long ago decided that she must leave South Africa to fulfil all her dreams. And over meals at her home, where she willingly waited at table, and over lemonades and steak dinners at the Holiday Inn in Bloemfontein, she had made up her mind that she was in the hands of people who were on a crusade to achieve her destiny.

Prowling with Anxiety

The days and nights of March before her departure from South Africa put an enormous strain on Zola. On the one hand she had to keep to her running schedule with appearances at tracks and official functions and as time shrank away, she knew hourly that she was coming to the precipice of a new life. But she could not confide the secret to anyone. Few teenagers would have been able to take the strain of waiting as calmly as she did. One day, when she had a pain in her stomach, her father explained that it was just knotted-up nerves. She had not been betraying any of her feelings on the outside, but absorbing it all inside her tiny frame.

The telephone lines to London from the Holiday Inn in Bloemfontein were red hot. Arrangements had to be made for the family's departure so that it would invite a minimum amount of comment or interference from the South African authorities, either sporting or government. As a therapy, Zola began compiling a diary of her thoughts.

Friday, 16 March

Today we had expected some news but there was none before my coach Pieter Labuschagne's BMW pulled up in the yard. My mother had complained that I had been prowling the house like a leopard for the past few days waiting to hear if there were any chance of Britain giving me a passport.

It was the waiting that was difficult. I'd made the decision. Now it was up to others so far away. We said nothing of it on the 120-mile drive to Kroonstad because we had my friend and training partner Elizna van Zyl with us. Nobody could know yet what we were planning. At least, not until we know one way or another if there is any chance.

She is running with me in the 800 metres tonight. Neither of us likes the distance. It is too quick for us. But there is a girl running who is a second or more faster than me and that will mean real opposition for once. I am not expecting too much because we've only done a week's training on the track to sharpen my speed. But Pieter's plan works. I take the lead from the start and 'kick' with two hundred metres to go.

My rival is with me there, but by the finish I am twenty metres clear. The time is very satisfying . . . 2 minutes 0.9 seconds, five seconds better than I've ever done before. Good old Kroonstad. Half this little farming town seems to have turned out. Pieter had thought about pulling me out of the race but hadn't dared. He reckons that there would be only 1000 spectators if I were not there. As it was more than 6000 turned up and there was a lot of atmosphere.

Pieter drove me home. Hardly had he left when the phone rang. Great news! London has said they will listen to my application if I go there.

Just a few more days now. It's something I've been dreaming of. Real races. I don't think I could have gone on much longer in South Africa. You need a reason to run and in the end beating the clock isn't enough. I was just running to beat times by girls I'd never met and never could meet. Except now there's a chance.

Saturday, 17 March

I phoned Pieter with the news. Then it's off to Johannesburg for a ninetieth anniversary dinner of the South African Amateur Athletic Union. Sydney Maree (the black South African runner now an American citizen) is there. That's a coincidence, because he's successfully changed his nationality.

I am presented with the 'Shield of Jove'. Apparently it's been gathering dust in a vault for twenty years because it is presented only to South Africans who achieve distinction in the Olympics. And they awarded it to me for 'my contribution to athletics'.

Rudolf Opperman, president of the Olympic Association, says I've succeeded in achieving more for South African athletics in 15 minutes 1.83 seconds, my world record, than two-and-a-half decades of concerted effort by officials. They didn't let me keep it. I suppose it's back in the vaults already. Instead I get to keep a huge stone on which an African artist has carved a picture of me running my world record. My father has the problem of carrying it home.

Sunday, 18 March

Lots of people point me out at the airport on the way home. I wonder how we'll ever leave South Africa without the whole world noticing.

Monday, 19 March

A team working for the South African Broadcasting Corporation arrive to make a documentary. They tried once before and now they want to do it again. We are all unhappy about it. My father refused to be interviewed. The rest of the day is not much better for them.

Tuesday, 20 March

Five-thirty in the morning, and the TV team are still with us, following me on my run. Finally we lose them. I think they realized we weren't cooperating, because they ask if they can come back another time. I wonder whether I will still be in South Africa to see them.

Wednesday, 21 March

My last track race in South Africa if all goes well. It's an inter-provincial championship in Port Elizabeth. I am running two races and there's just a chance that a girl in the 1500 metres will push me to a good time. The weather is perfect. No wind at all. But I'm on my own all the way again. The announcer is talking about big things, world junior record, four seconds faster than I've run before. Nice way to say goodbye.

Thursday, 22 March

The last full day, and we're travelling most of it. I've promised to run for a town called Welcom in a two-kilometre fun run through the streets. Pulling out will arouse suspicion.

Friday, 23 March

Today is the day. I am heartsore at saying goodbye to South Africa and at the thought that I won't run there again for a long time, perhaps never. But at least we are making an attempt now to get a British passport and that makes up for everything, even leaving my pets.

We get out through Johannesburg secretly. We just didn't want to be overwhelmed with the local journalists questioning us. I just wish all my friends had a chance of getting a passport that would let them run against the best in the world. Every athlete in South Africa dreams of it. It was terrible watching the world championships last year knowing that we could never be part of it. I am still not totally convinced I will be, but now everything looks a lot better.

Saturday, 24 March

We arrive at Amsterdam and the fly on to England. It is cold and wet but we have been praying for rain at home for months so how can we complain now? England's not unlike home, only the rain and the green are so different.

My coach has told me not to train until he arrives later, but I can't wait. I run this evening in a country lane, jumping out of the way of the cars as I go.

Zola takes to the Hampshire lanes

The Getaway

A blue BMW saloon nosed out of the long drive at the luxury home of Zola's uncle Ronnie and her journey to sporting happiness had begun. Zola decided to wear a new pair of chalk-striped black jeans and a pink, white and pale blue patterned sweater. She sat thoughtfully in the back seat behind steel spectacles.

Uncle Ronnie Evans, whose own father was born in Wales, was at the wheel. His wife Joyce, a former hospital nurse, and Frank Budd's sister, sat beside him in the front. Their destination as they turned out of Drakens Avenue in the fashionable hillside suburb of Roodeboort was Jan Smuts Airport, Johannesburg, forty minutes' drive away. It was the start of what Zola's family, South Africa, and most athletes in the world, believe to be the high road of her life.

Just ahead of Uncle Ronnie's car was a blue Toyota Cressida saloon with her father Frank at the wheel. He as usual was casually dressed in a light grey sweater with the letters 'G.R.' – 'No, it doesn't stand for George Rex,' he laughed – embroidered over his heart. He wore brown corduroys. His undistinguished outfit would hardly get him noticed by airport press photographers who had been patrolling the Jan Smuts airline counters for days for a possible unannounced departure of Zola, a heroine to the whole of sports-crazy South Africa.

Ahead of time, Frank had contacted the security people at the airport to say that he was going to Europe with Zola and wife Tossie but preferred anonymity as Zola had had enough of the spotlight from the press. It probably fooled none of them but it produced the security cloak they needed.

The Budd family were met in the security area of the airport, where they had arrived with five pieces of luggage, one brown and two black suitcases, a red shoulder bag and a black carry-on case. Their passports and luggage were taken from them and they were shown into the Royal Lounge which was conveniently empty of any other VIP travellers on this busy night.

Just ten minutes before Flight KL 594 took off at 5.30 p.m.

the Budds were shepherded into a black Mercedes saloon car and a security officer drove them 150 yards to the bottom of the first-class steps into the 747 Jumbo Jet. It was a gesture fit for a queen and that's the kind of adoration Zola enjoys among the young.

Zola and her parents sitting in Row 22 of the Business Class section, seats C, D, E, went unrecognized by the Dutch airline's hostesses as they served them a dinner of sole with sauté potatoes and a peach pie dessert on the Jumbo's leg between Johannesburg and Nairobi. Zola ate her dinner with relish. Though she weighs only 6 stone 2 pounds and stands 5 feet 2 inches in her bare feet, she has always had a healthy appetite.

The destination of Flight KL 594 was Schiphol Airport, Amsterdam, where a private 10-seater twin-engined Piper Chieftain aircraft chartered by the *Daily Mail* would be awaiting the party's arrival. On landing, the Budd family became 'Mr and Mrs Hamilton and Miss Hamilton' to hide their identities from prying pressmen who might have got a whiff of their departure from Johannesburg when it was too late. On the flight, Zola snatched a few hours sleep but she stayed awake to see the film *First Blood* starring Sylvester Stallone.

Eleven-and-a-half hours after takeoff Flight 594 rolled to a halt at Schiphol Airport as dawn was breaking around 6.00 a.m. During the all-night journey a 10-year-old South African boy travelling with his family had recognized Zola. His father approached Frank on the way out of the jetliner – 'Do you come from Bloemfontein? I think I know who you are.' Frank, usually the most affable of men, snapped his reply: 'In that case you'd better shut up about it.'

The *Mail* organization had gone like clockwork. The pilot of the newspaper's private aircraft, call-sign G-Boy, spoke by radio-telephone to the pilot of the KLM jetliner with a message for Mr Brian Vine to speak to the airline staff representatives when coming off the Jumbo. The airline had arranged to give VIP treatment to the Budd family, who were guided through the transit area to where private planes land and a forty-foot-long bus was laid on by KLM to get the party out to the Piper aircraft, parked close to the main runway.

One hour and ten minutes later the pilot, Captain Macey,

Above: Relaxing on KLM flight KL 594 en route from Johannesburg to Amsterdam and then a refuge near Southampton, England

Below: With her mother, Tossie, at the home of her aunt Joyce in Johannesburg, the night before she secretly flew to Europe

assured everyone on board the light plane that the White Cliffs of Dover were below, though the fluffy low cloud and heavy rain obscured this most famous of welcoming landmarks. Twenty minutes later, the Piper landed in a heavy rainstorm on a fully illuminated Southampton Airport runway. The flight had been organized with so much secrecy that the control tower had no knowledge of its arrival when taxed by casual inquirers.

Frank Budd proudly shows his British passport before landing at South-ampton from a private plane chartered by the *Daily Mail* to get the Budds from Holland to England

Zola, taking her first steps in Britain, actually ran towards the Customs and Immigration building, splashing through puddles in a new pair of brown suede zip-up boots, totally unusual footwear for a star whose hallmark is bare feet. She was home for the first time, to the land of her fathers and forebears, and despite the wet welcome her face was wreathed in smiles. She knew that Britain represented a sunnier horizon for her gift of being able to 'run a hole in the wind'.

A maroon Rover car carrying Frank and the luggage, and a Ford Orion with Zola and her mother aboard, snaked out of Southampton Airport after the passport and customs checks. The destination: a manor house in Brook on the edge of the New Forest. Zola appeared relaxed. She perked up in her car seat when she saw a cow or sheep in a field. She is besotted by animals of all kinds. The two-car convoy swung into the drive of the manor. It was the kind of place that no one would have thought to look for her. Unseen from the road, shrouded with trees, so peaceful you could hear bluebells tinkle.

It was to be her home for the next two weeks. These were days of anxiety for Zola, who had a whole international running career hanging on the whim of Home Secretary Leon Brittan, a brilliant lawyer whose name she had never heard before. To her diary next day, she committed her thoughts.

Zola stares reflectively through the windows of her first home in England, a flat near the New Forest

Sunday, 26 March

Two more training runs. But racing against the best in the world is what matters, whether or not it's in the Olympic Games: 1988 will be even more important for me when they have a 5000 metres on the programme. Target this year is to get into good races. I won't be worrying about times any more, only the opposition. I just hope the other British athletes are friendly. They can't realize what it has been like running on my own for so long.

Monday, 26 March

My application for a British passport is being delivered. By afternoon we hear it has been received and will be looked at 'sympathetically'. That's the best news I could have. I am dizzy thinking about it.

Now that the application for her British citizenship is with the Home Office, together with Frank Budd's British passport No. C981893 C issued by the British Consulate General in Johannesburg, the *Daily Mail* proudly reveals its vital role in bringing Zola to Britain. Says the newspaper on its front pages: 'Her father is British and she hopes to be in Britain's Olympic team in Los Angeles this year.'

'I have been brought up through my family to know about British history,' Zola said, 'and when I run in the Olympics I want to run for the country I feel is mine. I want to adopt Britain as my country and I would be proud to run for it.' The British Amateur Athletic Board Secretary Nigel Cooper spoke on ITN that night, saying Zola's arrival in Britain was 'great news – it is marvellous that this raw talent is coming here.'

Zola and her father felt that historical and sentimental attachments to Britain outweighed all the highly financially appealing offers from the United Sates. In South Africa Frank had begun the laborious process of establishing grounds for his daughter's citizenship. But inevitably, from 12,000 miles away, it was to be a long and complex process.

As Mr Budd explained: 'Given a straight choice we are 100 per cent in favour of the family settling in Britain and making our future life there. It would simply be going back to our roots and if you are going to represent a country then you should have that country's blood in your veins. We have family in Britain and that is the place we want to be. But in the end Zola must run against the world and we were prepared, reluctantly, to go to America or possibly even another country if that would be the door to international competition.'

As the result of this conversation and the clear intensity of the Budds' feelings for Britain and Zola's wish to run for this country, the *Mail* decided to bring the family to London, thus saving precious time and enabling her to train for the Olympics if selected. The International Olympic Committee rules state clearly that a naturalized citizen can run for his or her country as soon as a passport has been issued. But it was still a hard decision for the Budds. They were within a week of taking up an offer to go to a Californian university where Zola would be able to train with some of the best American athletes.

The American offers were solid. Emissaries had assured the Budd family that there would be no problem about her becoming an American citizen as several other South Africans have done. Although Zola was entitled to British citizenship because of her family, there was no guarantee that it would come in time for the Olympics. So the logical step was to come to England and make the application on the spot.

Editor Sir David English said: 'The *Daily Mail* firmly believes that Zola Budd will become a great British athlete. That is why we have helped her and her family to come to this country so that she can run for Britain – the country she wants to represent in world athletics. If she had remained in South Africa she would never have been able to compete in international events and so fulfil her full, astonishing athletic potential. That is why she decided to emigrate.

'As a British citizen she will be able to run against international competition and we felt it would be a tragedy if she had to run for any other country when her heart lies here. Bearing in mind the scale of sports scholarships being offered in America, the *Daily Mail* has decided to set up a legally constituted trust fund through the British Amateur Athletic Board so that Zola can run for Britain if she is granted citizenship.'

Newspapers in South Africa reacted sympathetically. The *Cape Argus* stated: 'She has gone to Britain to seek qualifications that will enable her to run in international competition, perhaps the Olympic Games. Who would blame her?'

The day after our announcement, the *Daily Mail* was able to publish the first picture of her running in Britain – stretching her sinewy legs on a country road. The athletics star who came to fame running in her bare feet, wore shoes, along with blue nylon running shorts and a white sweater. It was just after 7 a.m. on a chilly morning in Brook, Hampshire. Trying to stop Zola running, even in practice, is like trying to stop a runaway train. She has to exercise her limbs every day in the same way opera stars have to sing their scales.

At two minutes past seven she was on the road, even before the postman was on his rounds. A milkman in the village stopped and scratched his head as the bronze-legged star flashed past his stationary milk float. Two middle-aged joggers bundled up in warm track suits felt the breeze as the stripped-down Zola whistled by. They murmured a courteous 'good morning' without recognizing that they were running in world-class company.

Zola's coach, Pieter Labuschagne, was back in Bloemfontein still winding up his schooling duties prior to a spring and summer of advising her in Britain. He had told her over the telephone that she should take a rest while she waits for the Home Office decision on her citizenship application. But Zola, who has not missed a day's running since she was thirteen, said that she 'wouldn't feel right' without a run. 'But because of what Pieter says, I'm jogging only about two-and-a-half miles each day,' she said, making two miles sound like two yards.

From the conception of her decision to come to Britain, Zola had hoped and prayed that she would find lasting friendship and encouragement among British female athletes. Athletes can be bitchily competitive and by nature, runners are people whose nerves are strung out in order to drive the body through speed and stamina barriers. Hence they can be snappy creatures.

At first her arrival was welcomed by her peers. British international Debbie Peel, a rival of Zola's for an Olympic place said, 'I'm looking forward to the challenge of beating her. She will raise the standard of running in Britain.' Another star, Shirley Strong, said 'I'm all for her and good luck to the youngster. I hope she makes the Olympic team. Britain needs somebody like her. Let's face it, there's a lot of scope at that distance.'

Joyce Smith, ninth in the 1983 World Championship marathon, commented 'A lot of athletes born in other countries have competed for Britain and if Zola is granted a British passport there would be nothing to object to. But she has yet to prove herself here, of course.' The carping, though, was about to begin. It would puzzle the waif from the veldt. Not its anti-South African sentiments, but the fact that her sex could be so unfair as to suggest that a slower athlete should be preferred to a faster one, because the former had put more work in on her running! It didn't make sense.

Above: English village life includes donkeys, Zola discovers, as she keeps on training in Brook, Hampshire, a few days after her flight to Britain

Below: Zola, the political pawn, has a snapshot taken of herself and Parliament where days later she was the subject of discussion

Jane Furniss, a 3000-metre runner from the silverware city of Sheffield, believed her prospects were tarnished by Zola's sudden arrival on the British athletics scene. She admitted that she would not be the least disturbed if Zola got back on the next plane home. 'Even my Mum and Dad were a bit shocked, because normally I am not in the least outspoken. But I felt so strongly about it, I had to say exactly what I meant.' Jane explained that she had packed up her job as a dental nurse and lived on the dole in order to concentrate on clipping seconds off her best time for the 3000 metres, which she had reduced to 8 minutes 45 seconds. She had spent the last four years aiming at her Olympic goal and she felt bitter about Zola coming in to possibly sprint ahead of her with the selectors. Two months later Miss Furniss was to kiss Zola on the cheek in admiration after Zola, running barefoot, beat all-comers in the 1500 metres of the United Kingdom Championships at Cwmbran, South Wales, with a world junior record time of 4 minutes 4.39 seconds.

While Labour politicians carped too, with Doug Hoyle, the Labour MP for Warrington North, tabling a series of questions about Zola jumping the queue of citizenship applications, she got on with her practice twice a day. Those who sought to make Zola a politicall football had their game stopped when David Waddington, the immigration minister, admitted that her case had been given exceptional treatment because she was an athletic star. Mr Waddington called criticisms of the case rather petty and pointed out that some form of exceptional treatment had been given in the past to two black sportsmen applying for citizenship – the weightlifter from South Africa, Precious McKenzie, and the cricketer from Guyana, Alvin Kallicharran.

One Conservative Member of Parliament, Anthony Beaumont-Dark, spoke for the mood of much of Britain – judging by the letters' columns of the newspapers – when he said, 'If a country can't encourage a marvellous young girl like this, what can it do? She has every right to citizenship and these carping Labour people are just trying to ruin this young girl's life and her talent. They will use anything they can find to get at South Africa, even to the extent of jeopardizing the future of a young woman who wants to compete for Britain. They should be proud of her, rather than seeking to harm her. She has every chance of winning a gold medal for Britain and I for one hope she does.'

She was getting used to village life, nodding to the postman on her morning runs, and going with her father to buy groceries at the sub-post office. Her diary of those days was poignant.

Wednesday, 4 April

Everybody in the other flats has been very friendly. Father has made contact with several of them on his daily walks, and the friendship is to pay off when the newspapers finally track us to the house at Brook. The first warning comes in a call from the local sub-postmaster, who has had a call at his village shop from a South African journalist, asking whether a girl has been seen running through the village in recent days. Apparently, he has made the same check with every village in the New Forest, while following up a lead which I had inadvertently given of our whereabouts in a letter to a friend in Bloemfontein, Elizna van Zyl. I had mentioned we were living in a large house in a forest and this information had started an inquiry by a reporter from the *Cape Argus* throughout the New Forest. After all, I had entered Britain at Southampton – not far away. The sub-postmaster asked Pieter whether he wished to continue in low profile, but warned that the journalist seemed to know that we were in Brook.

Thursday, 5 April

Confirmation came first thing the next morning. Pieter and I were met on the gravel drive of the manor at 9 o'clock as I did my stretching exercises in preparation for the day's first training run. The journalist claimed to be a tourist who wanted my autograph for his daughter, but asked questions that made it obvious that he is more than he pretends. Finally, he took a small Instamatic camera from his pocket and shot two photographs of me before I set off.

Fortunately, the family were planning to move closer to Guildford that same day, but before our departure more journalists arrived. I spotted the 'strangers' from my bedroom and when the door was opened there was a ready answer awaiting them. 'You're six hours too late. The family have left,' the man from Radio Solent was told. Behind him were others from BBC Television and the *Daily Express*, but after a conference in the driveway the story seemed to have convinced them that their quarry had gone and they left. Five minutes later, the cars were packed and we moved to a hotel in Haslemere undetected.

Friday, 6 April

The tension is mounting. The family have convinced themselves that citizenship will come through today or not at all. We will be celebrating tonight or packing our bags for a miserable flight

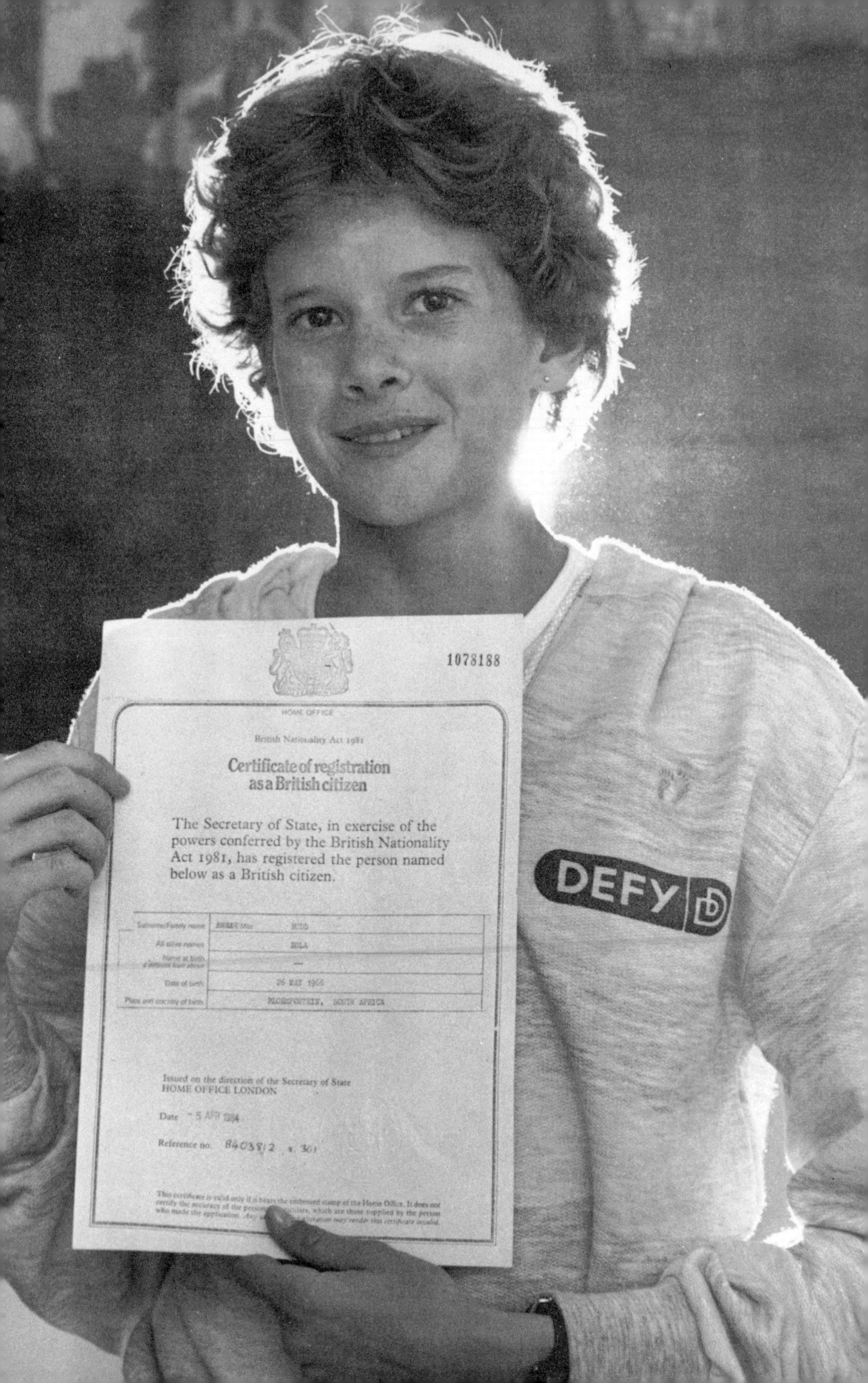

1078188

British Nationality Act 1981

Certificate of registration as a British citizen

The Secretary of State, in exercise of the powers conferred by the British Nationality Act 1981, has registered the person named below as a British citizen.

Surname/Family name	BUDD	Mrs/Miss	MISS
All other names	ZOLA		
Name at birth, if different from above	—		
Date of birth	26 MAY 1966		
Place and country of birth	BLOEMFONTEIN, SOUTH AFRICA		

Issued on the direction of the Secretary of State
HOME OFFICE LONDON

Date 5 APR 1984

Reference no. B403812 × 301

This certificate is valid only if it bears the embossed stamp of the Home Office. It does not certify the accuracy of the personal particulars, which are those supplied by the person who made the application. Any false statement or misrepresentation may render this certificate invalid.

DEFY

home. I train for about eight miles in the morning, but the rest of the day is spent in anxious and impatient waiting in my room. There is one other appointment. Lord and Lady Onslow, whose estate borders the Merrow Park home that we will move into if citizenship is granted, have invited me to use their extensive grounds for my training, and want me to meet them for a lunchtime drink. His Lordship drives Pieter and myself around the estate, calculating distances and working out where I can run.

The trip breaks up the day, but does nothing to dispel the tension. Finally, at 4.30 comes the call from London to say that the citizenship papers have been issued. At 5.50, a messenger arrives to deliver them. It's champagne all round for everybody except me. I never drink any alcohol. I'm more concerned with the whereabouts of my pet canary, left behind in the flat in the New Forest during the rushed departure the previous day. Within minutes, Britain's newest citizen leaves the party behind to train in the hotel grounds.

Left: Zola gets her certificate of citizenship and does not disguise her happiness at being British

Looking after her first English pet, a white budgerigar, bought in a Bournemouth pet shop

Opposite above: Zola listens intently to the expert she trusts most, her coach Pieter Labuschagne, on the grass at Crystal Palace

Below: Stretching at Crystal Palace – getting an upside-down view of her world

Above: Pieter Labuschagne sets his stop-watch in practice at Crystal Palace

Saturday, 7 April

It's moving day again to the third 'home' since our arrival only a fortnight ago. This time, it's to the house in Merrow Park, where eventually Pieter and his wife Caren will live. For now, he will stay in an hotel, the White Horse, while we use his house until our own becomes vacant.

But before we leave for Guildford, I insist that I do my normal training run which today lasts nearly an hour and covers almost fourteen kilometres. By mid-afternoon, it would be easy to mistake us for any other English family on a housing estate as Dad happily mows his new lawn.

Sunday, 8 April

Now I have British citizenship, I need a British athletic club, and there have been several offers including one from Britain's leading track club, Wolverhampton and Bilston. But Pieter and I want a club closer to our Guildford base and feelers have been put out to Aldershot, Farnham and District, a Hampshire club with a reputation for middle-distance runners. Today, Pieter has arranged to meet Beryl Aston, who runs the women's section there, and her husband Gerry, to discuss it. They accept me with delight and promised a committee meeting on Tuesday to confirm it formally.

They also promise to arrange a race for me at Dartford in Kent, the following Saturday, when I run as a guest during a Southern League match. It's all good news for Pieter, who has been keen to get on with the business of 'producing' me.

There are problems for him when he returns home – I'm in tears. I'm missing the South African junior championships that weekend, where I would have been competing and where all my old friends would be. He tells me to look forward to my first race in Britain and I'm already consoled. Running races is all I dream about.

A pensive Zola contemplates a practice run at Crystal Palace

74

Dartford—Her First Run as a Briton

There was an air of anxiety in the *Daily Mail* offices on the two days before Zola was to put herself to the test in her first competitive race outside South Africa. It wasn't the thought of 'will she, won't she' come through with the kind of performance that would keep the public's faith. The expectation of a fine performance was the thrilling part of the planning. The newspaper, which has a firm agreement with Zola and her coach to keep well away from all the decisions about where, how and what she runs, was not even overly anxious about the choice of venue, even though a *Times* headline had described the Dartford Harriers' council track in Kent as 'dangerous'.

The choice of Dartford was hers and her coach's prerogative. The *Mail* executives felt an overriding responsibility for her safety, because of the baying of the Left wing and the frustration and envy of the rest of Fleet Street that a major newspaper had won her trust and the rights to the first-person account of her new career. Sir David English asked his senior men on the Zola Budd story to ensure that the right precautions were taken to avoid a melee. Her first press conference should be arranged so that reporters and the TV audience at home would start to get to know her as a personality.

It was decided that she would be brought to the track with Pieter in a car driven by Neil Wilson, who would be covering the meeting for the *Mail* from the athletics point of view. Behind would come a car bringing her parents. There would be no question of doing her pre-race warming up at the Dartford track because of the sheer numbers of the expected press who might unsettle her before her debut.

Normally, about 150 people would come to watch an athletics meeting at Central Park, Dartford: mostly interested parties, relatives of the runners, spouses or friends. At midday, with the

At last, Zola's face says it all – I'm British and proud of it. I have my passport – now where's the competition!

77

Zola faces her first press conference, after racing at Dartford: on her extreme right, the author (Brian Vine), on her left, her coach Pieter Labuschagne, her father (standing) and her mother, Tossie

Right: Setting sail for home at Dartford

Zola race still three hours away, it looked as if the police precautions might have been unnecessary. But as the minutes ticked by a river of people started flowing across the grass and eventually encompassed the red cinder track for which Zola was putting on spikes for the first time for years. There was a sense of occasion in the air. A feeling that perhaps this would be a day to tell your grandchildren about.

As the *Guardian* athletics writer put it on the Monday following: 'Zola Budd's opening strides on the shale of Central Park, Dartford, have run her firmly into contention for British Olympic selection ...' Her time, 9 minutes 2.06 seconds, on that spring afternoon was inside the Olympic qualifying standard and a junior British record. It was a stupendous effort when one considered that it was only the third time in her career she had run on a non-all-weather surface and the first time she had ever run 3000 metres in spikes. Together with the fact that she was lionized like a gladiator entering the Coliseum in Rome. A posse of shirt-sleeved police officers had to cut a path for her through a wire fence and past spectators obscuring the track, after she shoed herself, sitting on rough lumps of dark earth.

Neil Wilson wrote in the *Mail:* 'Zola Budd did not set important British records on the track at her first attempt but the 5000 spectators attracted to Dartford's Central Park provided record enough. It was the biggest crowd yet for a Southern League athletics meeting by a mile.

'On her first public appearance in her new country, Zola was cheered round the track and off it. For three weeks her name had been public property around the world. Never can any

Above: At her first race Zola carries off a bouquet

Opposite above: About to pass at Dartford on the tip of her toe

Below: Zola lines up at Dartford, with the help of policemen called in to control the track's biggest-ever crowd

runner have been under such pressure while turning out for just a club fixture. Mind you, it was hard to recognize what took place as club athletics. It was an event.

'There was David Coleman live around Britain, an NBC television crew from America, and a vast array of cameras more accustomed to being focused on a Diana than a Zola. There was a police escort, and a joker with a sense of occasion fed strains of the *Chariots of Fire* theme music into the public address system.

' "Look, it's Zola," shouted one delighted little girl who three weeks ago would never have heard of her. The crowd took up the cry. There was a bouquet of flowers from a rival club, a present of a T-shirt and sweater in club colours from her Aldershot team-mates and so many pats on the back she was only safe on the track.

Zola is escorted through the Dartford crowd

'The Mayor of Dartford came too, complete with gold chain of office, and with him the chairman of the Leisure Services Committee, anxious to hear something nice said about his controversial track. Of carping politicians, there was no sign. The only speech made in Central Park spoke of the "pride and pleasure with which we welcome to Dartford and to British athletics Zola Budd".

'The girl in the spotlight did not put a foot wrong. Her run over 3000 metres was the best answer she knew to her critics. A time of 9 minutes 2.6 seconds is not world-shattering by any standards and certainly not by her own. But it was all her coach had decreed and enough by a margin of 2.4 seconds to save her the further bother of having to run again to qualify for consideration for Olympic selection.

Time for a belly laugh after her record time at Dartford

'Diplomatically, Zola refused to speculate on how much Dartford's much-criticized cinder track had slowed her first steps towards Olympic honours. "I wouldn't have been any faster at Crystal Palace because I didn't plan to run any faster," she said. Of course, Saturday's opposition was no stronger than she had left behind in her native country. She lapped four of them but she accepts that the best comes later.

'Within an hour of arrival, she was gone, forgetfully leaving her glasses and running shoes behind. It was all she lost all day. Her club won the match. She celebrated on the way home with a cuppa in a tearoom in Dorking High Street. She had to walk barefoot to that. It made her day complete.'

Coach and star share a secret at Dartford, where Zola reported to coach Pieter Labuschagne after her record-breaking debut

Opposite above: Getting into her stride at a practice run at Crystal Palace

Below: With British Amateur Athletic Board officials Nigel Cooper and Marea Hartman at the Hurlingham Club

Zola was hardly puffing when she made her way to an orange tent at the side of the track where a press conference for her was convened by the Dartford Harriers. The club's commentator, Geoffrey Wightman, son of the club president, introduced Zola to the throng which threatened at one stage to burst through the sheep-pen fencing that had been hurriedly erected to protect her from a mobbing. She sipped orange juice from a paper cup and fielded her first questions from a formidable array of British reporters. Meanwhile, cameramen popped up from behind her to take as many candid pictures as time would allow. To little Zola this seemed worse than facing an exam paper on political science after running 10,000 metres but she managed to crack one joke before being directed to stand inside the tent while the broad shoulders of the law formed a human funnel for her exit from the track and into a waiting car, which had a police escort.

Zola was the last one to be impressed by the film-star treatment. She is used to stepping off a track in South Africa and walking with a friend to the next open space for a picnic. But as she clutched her yellow and blue floral bouquet she began to accept that Britain was not Kroonstad and that she was now a public personality, like the tennis teenagers, Maureen 'Little Mo' Connolly of the 1950s, the young Bjorn Borg, Chrissie Evert and Tracey Austin. And British athletics has seemed to be crying out overlong for a girl genius whom every housewife could mother.

Zola returns to the street where her grandfather Frank was born, Rushmore Road, London E5, the pebble-dashed house on the left

Going to See Her Roots

More valuable than the deeds to his farm is the blood-red birth certificate of his father that Frank Budd carries around with him. It had been the proof of his ancestry that earned him a passport and provided Zola with the wherewithal to become an international athlete. For the granting of citizenship to Frank was the reason he was able to invoke the British Nationality Act Section 3 (I) which allows the Home Secretary discretion to give nationality to minors of British citizens.

Though he had been in England many times on holiday trips, Frank had never bothered to look up his father's birth certificate. He knew *when* he was born, if not exactly where. It was only when it became an immeasurably important piece of documentary proof for his own citizenship rights that he put feelers out to secure a certified copy of his father's birth registration in the files of the General Register Office in London. Those files sit today in St Catherine's House, a modern version of the old Somerset House on the corner of Kingsway and Aldwych, less than a mile from the *Daily Mail*'s Northcliffe House headquarters.

Application No. G2161 by the *Daily Mail* produced not only a copy of the vital certificate, but also the first news Frank had of *where* his father was born: 129 Rushmore Road, Lower Clapton, in London's East End.

It was right and proper that as soon as the family had a chance they should visit the house where granddad was born and which had meant so much in bringing them to Britain. Granddad had been very fond of Tossie, Frank's wife, who used to cook for him in Bloemfontein when he became bedridden. He rang her up the day before he died to thank her for all she had done for him. He had never bothered to learn a word of Afrikaans in the half century he spent in South Africa but he was universally loved by the townspeople, most of whom speak Afrikaans as their first language.

That morning after her debut at Dartford, Zola, her parents and Pieter headed for London by car on a pilgrimage to see where the Zola Budd story really began. Rushmore Road in

87

Lower Clapton is an unremarkable street of terraced Victoriana. The people who live there tell you with pride that many of them are Cockney born and bred. Like the Cockneys themselves the street hasn't changed much in the 112 years of its existence.

Zola walked down that street, eyes wide behind big spectacles to look for number 129 where a baby boy was born, and christened Frank George Budd. Frank was still alive when Zola was born. He died sixteen years ago at eighty-two. Zola hoped to see inside the house that was once his home.

It was a highly emotional experience and for the visit back to her roots Zola put on what would have been known as her Sunday best when this part of the world was in its heyday: red woollen trousers and jacket to match, with a pink silk blouse.

'I can't really remember granddad because I was only nineteen months when he died,' she said, moments before the door at number 129 swung open in the sunshine. 'But my mother has always told me what a wonderful man he was to the family and I have always wanted to find out where his life began.' The old Budd house in Rushmore Road has spiritedly shrugged off the unhappiness of wars and hardships from well before the Boer War through two world wars. It is a testament to that part of London.

The knock on the door was answered by Alf Rogers, who had just fed his three Irish collie dogs, Lassie, Prince and Queenie. 'Little Lassie', a miniature collie, barked a welcome in the background. Alf recognized Zola at once but couldn't understand what she was doing on his doorstep. When she shyly explained about her grandfather, Alf gave her a great friendly welcome.

'That's wonderful,' he said. 'You've got to come in. Fancy your family coming from round here. Blimey you're famous you are! I saw you on the telly. I thought you were really great. Thank God you're on our team. You were smashing. Now come on in.' Zola went in and was given the grand tour of the spick-and-span little house. She met all the animals, the dogs and a white and ginger cat, and Alf's son, Michael, a local dustman.

'It's so strange,' she said. 'I've often tried to visualize what granddad's house would be like. It's as if I've seen it in a dream some time before in my life. I feel I know it somehow.' The visit was even more emotional for Zola's father. 'It's quite something to stand here in my father's old home,' he said. 'A strange feeling comes over me. I almost sense his presence as a young man. I've always been drawn to find my roots in bricks and mortar.'

Granddad Budd died in Bloemfontein. The old parchment-coloured bricks of the terraced house have now been pebble-dashed by proud Alf and the traditional lace curtains at the old Budd windows were as white as the White Cliffs of Dover.

Top: Zola greeted on the doorstep of her granddad's London home by the present owner, Alf Rogers. Zola's father beside her was seeing his father's home for the first time, too

Zola strokes a cat in her granddad's old home

Zola was pensive as she walked up Rushmore Road on the sunny side of the street. Frank George Budd had brought sunshine into her life nearly a quarter of a century after his death! That Sunday was a day out for Zola looking around London. She went to Petticoat Lane and to a local pub. With the race out of the way and with the qualifying time for the Olympic trial now on the records, Zola was relaxed. She was able to talk about her first few weeks in Britain.

First of all, she dismissed all the stories of her being lured here. 'Where do they get these ideas?' she asked. 'I wanted to come to Britain and I wanted to run in Britain. Now it's happened, why should I be unhappy? It's not up to me whether I run for Britain, but of course I'd like to. I'd like to run in the Olympics, too, but for now I'm just pleased to be here and allowed to run.

'People keep telling me I must be under terrible pressure. But it's no different to back home in South Africa, and here, at least, I'm not the only athlete they know. Once I've run a few races and the novelty's worn off, I am sure everybody will treat me like any other athlete in Britain. Of course, I felt pressure on Saturday, but not from the press or the crowd. The pressure on me was to run well on my first appearance here but, in fact, I didn't feel any more nervous than usual. I enjoyed it.

'It was so much better controlled than in South Africa, that it was easier for me to get on with the competition. Nobody made me come to Britain. It was my decision. I'm here because I want to be, and I plan to be here for a long time, not just this summer. Of course, I shall always visit South Africa. It's where my family are. I shall go back there this autumn for my brother's wedding. I'll probably train there for some of the English winter. But that doesn't mean I'm not a permanent resident here. I'm British now ... and I'm beginning to feel British.'

While waiting for her papers to be processed, she had stayed the whole while in her New Forest lair. 'It rained and rained every day,' said Zola. 'I thought, "Does it never stop in this country?" I train early in the morning. So there I was going out running at 7 o'clock and the ground and grass would be absolutely white with frost. I had to buy a long-sleeved shirt to keep my arms warm and a pair of gloves for my hands. But it was a very beautiful time. And so quiet and peaceful.

Top: Zola on a Sunday outing at Britain's most popular tourist spot, Buckingham Palace

Middle (left to right): Feeding the pigeons in Trafalgar Square with Dad, Frank, keeping a watchful eye – he keeps pigeons on their farm in South Africa. One champ greets another when Zola shook hands with fellow guest, ex-heavyweight boxing champion Henry Cooper at the British Olympics Ball at Grosvenor House, London. In a London TV studio, a congratulatory peck from coach Pieter Labuschagne when Zola received her Sporting Personality 1983–84 award, earned in South Africa. She spoke over a satellite television transmission.

Bottom: Trading in Petticoat Lane market for souvenirs

'That's one of the things I like so much here. The grass. There's so much of it you can run on. We found a beautiful stretch one day but I didn't realize it was part of a golf course. We were running down what turned out to be the fairway, wondering why the people at the far end were standing watching us so intently. It turned out they were waiting to drive off and we were directly in their path. But even then they were very pleasant and friendly.' Zola went on: 'That's applied everywhere we've gone. British people are friendly. They call out "Hello" or "Nice to see you here" in the street. And they all smile.'

And Zola Budd is smiling too.

Relaxing after her Oslo race – a portrait in glasses

Zola Will Beat Them All

It was a warm night last March at the University of Port Elizabeth track when Brian Vine stood alongside the *Mail*'s athletics expert, Neil Wilson, to see Zola run for the first time.

Her riveting display of long-striding grace and gritty determination had wholly impressed Neil. He later committed to paper his emotions of that night.

'Zola Budd should not expect her path to the top to be easy. But I believe her potential is at least greater than Mary Decker's. There will come a day when she is not just mentioned in the same breath, but mentioned first.'

Zola Budd's best times last winter would have ranked her eleventh in the world at 3000 metres, her target event for the Olympic Games. She would have ranked fourteenth at 1500 metres and, of course, first at 5000 metres, an event at which she holds the unofficial world record. Her best times are:

300 metres	2:00.9	
1000 metres	2:37.9	world junior record
1500 metres	4:01.81	world junior record, South African senior record
3000 metres	8:37.5	world junior and South African records
5000 metres	15:01.83	world senior record
10,000 metres	32:00.23	fifth fastest ever run and South African record
10 km road	32:00.20	South African record

Vine and Wilson knew they were watching greatness in the making. Wilson says that on that March night in Port Elizabeth his thoughts were transported immediately back to a cold afternoon at RAF Cosford in Staffordshire seven years beforehand. That was when he had his first real sighting of Sebastian Coe, with that lightness of foot, that floating movement, that long stride on slim, sinewy legs.

Zola runs between cars on the streets of Oslo

'The excitement I felt watching Coe was alive in me again as Zola, slender and seventeen years old, sped around the track. I knew I was watching someone with the potential to become one of the greatest women athletes the world has known. To say Zola Budd could be good is like saying Steve Cram has promise. Nature blessed her with so many talents but fate dictated she was born in South Africa, the one place on earth excluded from international running competition.'

Now she has British citizenship, there is nothing more to stop Zola achieving all that the Coes, Crams and Ovetts have for this country. 'How good is she now? Her best times this winter would have ranked her the fastest in Britain last year at 1500, 3000 and 5000 metres and the third fastest at 800 metres. At both 1500 and 3000 metres only one British girl has ever run faster. And remember, Zola is still only seventeen.

'It becomes barely believable when you hear from her coach that for the past two years he has been restricting her training to hold her back. "If I let her do what she could have been doing, what would it have achieved?" he asks. "What's the sense of her just lapping the other South African runners twice in a race instead of once?"'

94

Up with the greats in the Oslo 10-kilometre race, her first international contest in British colours, Zola, with Grete Waitz (centre) and Ingrid Kristiansen. Ingrid won by seventeen seconds from Zola, who was third

Indeed, he barely bothers her with track training, which other runners use to sharpen their speed. Before running 800 metres recently five seconds faster than she had ever run it before, she had trained on a track just twice. Of course, some of those who have never seen her train or race are casting doubts on her chances in the tougher world of top-class competition outside South Africa. They say she in inexperienced in races against girls as good as she is. They say she will be cut to pieces running barefoot. They say she is a one-paced runner who may break records but will not win races.

Neil's answer is this: of course she is inexperienced. She is the first to admit it. But then, so are all 17-year-olds and few have ever had such a talent as hers. 'Right now I'll wager a Krugerrand to an old halfpenny that, given approval from the International Olympic Committee, she will win a place in Britain's team for 3000 metres in the Los Angeles Games this year, she will reach the final, and once there, anything is possible, even a gold medal.

'I'll go further and bet she will be odds-on favourite for gold in the 1988 Olympics, when 5000-metre and probably 10,000-metre races for women are added to the programme.'

Shortly afterwards Wilson was able to record a further achievement by Zola, racing to a new British junior record for

1500 metres at Crystal Palace on 26 April 1984. Wilson reported: 'Zola's time of 4 minutes 10.82 seconds was four seconds inside the previous British junior 1500-metre record set six years ago. It has blasted open the door to next month's UK championships at Cwmbran by being nearly fourteen seconds inside the qualifying standard.'

However, the carping goes on. Criticism of Zola running barefoot hardly deserves dismissal. Has everyone forgotten Bruce Tulloh? He ran barefoot for Britain and won the European 5000 metres title in 1962. He was as frail-looking as Zola and nobody stood on his feet. And one-paced? So far, yes. She has the ability to cruise, like a car in fifth gear, effortlessly and efficiently. In her world-record 5000 metres, she lapped the track twelve times as regular as clockwork.

But don't let that deceive anybody. She has a turn of speed when she needs one. In her most recent 800 metres her rival, a girl who had run the distance nearly two seconds faster than Zola, was level with her with 200 metres to go. At the finish Zola was 20 metres ahead, having run the last 200 metres in just twenty-nine seconds. Of course, things can go wrong. Zola is a near-18-year-old with the body of a 14-year-old. She has more developing to do and that could change her.

She is also a shy, withdrawn girl who is happiest with her animals and with athletes, and she is unlikely to cope well with the extreme pressures her success would bring down on her. 'She expresses herself only with her legs,' is how Pieter sums up the Zola magic.

Zola stops for a broadcast interview after running third to Ingrid Kristiansen and the great Grete Waitz in a 10-kilometre race through the streets of Oslo in May